Praise for David Magee and *Dear William*

"[David Magee] is an incredible talent and he has written an incredible book."

—Elizabeth Vargas, host, *Heart of the Matter* podcast

"Many struggle with hidden addictions and resulting pain, and this book can help them before it is too late. Every student and parent will benefit."

—Dr. Victor Boschini, Chancellor, TCU

"Essential, poignant, and insightful reading for anyone aiming to understand . . . patterns of addiction."

—Kirkus Reviews

"David Magee connects with parents and students on the topic of substance misuse and personal responsibility like few people I have witnessed. He started a movement . . . and he hasn't let up since—inspiring students and parents as a speaker and starting a university wellness center. His voice resonates with vulnerability and common-sense, with a story every parent and every student can learn from."

—Brandi Hephner LaBanc, Vice Chancellor for Student Affairs, University of Massachusetts

D1518212

Things Have Changed

Also by David Magee

Dear William

THINGS HAVE CHANGED

What Every Parent (and Educator) Should Know About the Student Mental Health and Substance Misuse Crisis

DAVID MAGEE

Matt Holt Books
An Imprint of BenBella Books, Inc.
Dallas, TX

This book is not intended to be a substitute for the medical advice of a licensed counselor or physician. The reader should consult with their mental health professional in any matters relating to their health or the health of a child.

Things Have Changed copyright © 2023 by David Magee

Matt Holt is an imprint of BenBella Books, Inc.
10440 N. Central Expressway
Suite 800
Dallas, TX 75231
benbellabooks.com
Send feedback to feedback@benbellabooks.com

BenBella and *Matt Holt* are federally registered trademarks.

Printed in the United States of America
10 9 8 7 6 5 4 3 2 1

Library of Congress Control Number: 2022060013
ISBN 9781637743966 (trade paperback)
ISBN 9781637743973 (electronic)

Editing by Katie Dickman
Copyediting by Jennifer Brett Greenstein
Proofreading by Madeline Grigg and Marissa Wold Uhrina
Text design and composition by Jordan Koluch
Cover design by Brigid Pearson
Printed by Lake Book Manufacturing

Special discounts for bulk sales are available.
Please contact bulkorders@benbellabooks.com.

For my three children: William, Hudson, and Mary Halley.
One lost the battle, but two are battling and winning.
This book is for your children and all the children everywhere
so they can find and keep joy as you have.
Here's hoping it helps spare so many the pain that broke us,
leading them toward the hope that healed us.

Throughout this book I share anecdotal stories of different students and families to help illustrate what they face. Each of these stories are true, drawn from engagement with students and families throughout the country, but the names, locations, and other identifying characteristics have been changed.

Contents

INTRODUCTION

We want so much better for our children, those we parent and those we teach. It's what we think about and work so very hard at almost every day. Yet we've left the children behind just when they need us most. Really, we have.

That's because this generation of students is struggling with substance misuse and mental health issues like never before, facing anxiety, depression, suicide ideation, and eating disorders in startling numbers. They desperately need our help to manage the crisis. For many in this generation, it's now a matter of life and death. For the rest, it's a matter of finding and keeping the joy they deserve, the joy that mental health and substance misuse issues often steal.

Consider that the U.S. Centers for Disease Control (CDC) issued a recent warning, revealing data showing that 44 percent of students "felt sad or hopeless during the past year." The U.S. surgeon general recently issued an advisory on youth mental health, suggesting the problem is so severe that the "future well-being of our country depends on how we support and invest in the next generation."

These facts speak the loudest, though: accidental drug over-dose deaths in teens and those in their early twenties are rising sharply, and so are deaths by suicide. That's because things have changed so drastically and so fast that many, a majority per-haps, are struggling to navigate the rigors of daily life, including school, extracurriculars, friends, and family, even if they don't have mental health and substance abuse issues. They'll smile and tell us they are okay because that's what we want to hear, but no, they are not okay.

Yes, America. We have a problem—our children are hurting and at significant risk, and we must get better at how we en-gage, guide, and educate them.

You'd think that in our country, a global leader in edu-cation and innovation, we'd be better at guiding and teach-ing students, given the life-changing facts we know. There's no shortage of research revealing what students face in men-tal health and substance misuse issues and the most effective solutions. We know, for instance, that students better face life's challenges with more sleep and that social media like In-stagram increases the likelihood of eating disorders in teens. Yet, despite countless research findings, students today face a mental health and substance use disorder crisis like never be-fore, making it obvious that critical, life-changing—and even life-*saving*—information is not reaching students and families. That's because research conclusions alone are not enough. We must share the information with students, parents, and educa-tors in an engaging way.

That's where I enter this story. I am among the few stu-dent wellbeing activists who have been conducting face-to-face mental health and substance misuse educational talks in schools and universities in recent years. More than once, I was the first speaker to appear before the entire student body in over two years—since the pandemic began. Even amid large audiences, sometimes more than a thousand students gathered in a gymnasium or auditorium, I could tangibly see their pain, often illustrated by tears streaming down cheeks. After hearing my "Things Have Changed" school talk, many parents, educators, and students asked if I would turn it into a book, which could help them combat this epidemic by providing a clear map outlining the challenges faced and their potential solutions.

This book is my response. It is not an assignment I sought. No, this job found me. I planned to finish my career in traditional media, managing news sites or a more diversified content organization. But that's what happens with a calling—it finds us.

My journey began in personal and family crises. Suffering from my own substance use disorder—prescription Adderall from a doctor and alcohol—I lost my marriage and career in my midforties. Then, my oldest son, William, an honors college student and track athlete, died of an accidental drug overdose not long after graduating from college; my middle child, Hudson, nearly died of an accidental drug overdose in college (he was found blue and not breathing with no heartbeat at a fraternity house on campus, though he awoke from a coma two days later without brain damage); and my daughter, Mary Halley, struggled with an eating disorder beginning in high school and continuing into college. All this tragedy and crisis occurred in our family within several years, shattering us into pieces.

On the day I found our William dead, with so much love and promise gone with his last breath, my hands shook and my stomach quivered with nausea. As word spread, almost everyone who knew us thought this would be more than our broken family could take.

But don't feel sorry for me or my family.

Yes, we lost our William and miss him every day, and will for as long as we get to see the sunrise. But I got back my marriage, my career, and my joy, thanks to determined recovery. Our son Hudson got his life and joy back as well; after his near death, he got sober at twenty-one and has remained in recovery for more than a decade. And our daughter is now years into eating disorder recovery and a married mother of three. We all draw strength from William, individually and collectively, as if some of the best parts of his departing soul were divided among us, making us stronger to battle.

We don't want other students and families to suffer as we did. That's why three years after William died, I wrote the newspaper column "For Ole Miss Freshmen: My Son William's Story" in the *Oxford Eagle*, the small daily that I published (Oxford is the hometown of the University of Mississippi, which William and Hudson attended, as did my wife and I.) The newspaper averaged just five thousand unique readers per day. Still, my column about how William thought he could use substances including alcohol, cocaine, and marijuana in college and just walk away at graduation, but then ended up with a problem he couldn't manage, went viral and was read by more than one million people. We used the momentum to help start the William Magee Center for AOD and Wellness Education on the University of Mississippi campus, designed to help students with substance misuse. The effort put me in regular contact with students, many of whom talked openly and honestly about what they faced, deepening my learning and bolstering my calling.

Since William's story was just a part of our family's saga of addiction, recovery, love, and loss, I wrote the memoir *Dear William*, my first book in over a decade, baring the depths of our pain and reclamation of joy. I didn't know what to expect, honestly. They like to say in publishing that only celebrities can write a successful memoir these days. Yet a crowd of more than seven hundred came to the November book launch, and momentum spread across the winter the way kudzu grows in these parts in summer. The *CBS Mornings* show came calling—yes, that was Gayle King and noted senior reporter Jim Axelrod talking about our story on national TV. Parents and teachers read *Dear William* and told school board members and administrators about it. Soon, one invitation after another came, from New Jersey to Texas to the Mississippi Delta, for me to speak to students.

I struck a nerve, writing as a nobody yet speaking in a voice for everybody—the students, parents, and educators throughout this nation, engulfed in this crisis without help or acknowledgment, like people being held underwater and being told to breathe as if nothing were happening at all. That's why I've devoted my career to this work, advocating for students and families facing mental health challenges and substance misuse.

Everyone in the vital student ecosystem needs more understanding about what's happening and how to help students fight back. The effort starts with parents, educators, and health care professionals. That's why I wrote this book mainly for parents but also for educators and everyone who can help us help the middle, high school, and college students who so need it. It's about how *things have changed* and what you can do about it; it's about giving our young people their best odds for joy and wellbeing and the help and guidance they need and deserve.

Frankly, I never thought I'd write this book. I remember that the first time I walked into a school to give a speech about how things have changed, a student asked me if I was there "to give us a drug talk," and I was thinking, *No, oh goodness, no, I'm not that person.* I never wanted to be that person. I tried to run from it, even. But this job found me because, yes, I am that person. I crawled across the floor, then got myself back up, and got myself and my family back into living joyous lives, despite our significant loss. Once there, students and parents came with questions. How did you save yourself? How did you handle losing a child? How did your other son find success in recovery? What do you wish you'd known when your children were in middle school or in high school? How would you handle a struggling college student who doesn't want help? Is fentanyl indeed everywhere?

So many good questions, so many hurting students deserving answers. Indeed, I have lived through our family's breakage and repair, and from that experience I have built engagement with students and families facing similar problems and seeking solutions for the mental health and substance misuse crisis. So here I am, trying to make the problem clear, as frightening as it may be, connecting the dots from technology to fentanyl, fostering communication between parents and children, and showing that we can change things, for your child and for all children. That's the half-full glass that energizes me to do this work. That's the half-full glass that must motivate you to dig in as well. Your children need and deserve it.

1

THE JOY FACTOR

How we need to communicate with teens and college students is so specific that they'll tune us out if we miss the mark by just a bit. The adult-to-youth dialogue that seems relatively easy when children are eight, nine, or even ten years old, when they still consider adults wise and humorous, becomes problematic when they reach puberty. The challenge doesn't subside for most young people until late in college, if not beyond. And attempting to connect on the most sensitive, personal subjects, like mental health and substance misuse, is even more difficult.

Yet, if we can figure out how to meet students where they are on these sensitive subjects by speaking the correct language, a jackpot of engagement awaits. But it's on us, not them, to figure that out.

I bring this up at the beginning of this book because our struggle to communicate with students is a frequent obstacle to the education and support they need and is the foundation of the anxiety and depression they experience. That's because the lack of engagement can leave them feeling locked off and lonely when they need it most. We know, for instance, that talk therapy is an essential aspect of mental health, yet for students facing our fast-moving, complicated world, engagement around their feelings doesn't come easy.

They don't have the time (racing through the school day, after-school activities, and everything else in between), much less the emotional aptitude (considering their central nervous system is still rapidly developing), to be told what they are uncomfortable hearing or even to initiate discussions. They can become deeply emotional but have difficulty expressing emotion.

We can indeed reach them, though. I learned this from trial and error in the field, speaking to student groups, including schools and social organizations. Initially, I'd get introduced as someone who was there to talk to them about alcohol and drugs. I'd pass the first test, showing humility and relatability by explaining how I'd struggled with depression, self-medicating with Adderall and alcohol, before finding recovery. I'd also share how my children battled anxiety and depression, self-medicated substance misuse (my sons), and an eating disorder (my daughter) before one died and two found recovery. Next, I'd tell students about the risks they face, *how things have changed* since their parents and teachers were teens, and what they can do about it. Educators told me that the response from students was very good. The majority appeared to listen, some had questions, and a few even sought counseling or treatment immediately after.

"Remarkable," a principal told me. "We've never had that kind of response to an alcohol and drug talk. It's your humility, I think, and they can relate because you aren't talking down to them."

People will tell a speaker what the speaker wants to hear.

But I believed the hype, considering myself good at talking to students, because invitations continued.

I'd been a communicator for most of my professional life, writing, editing, speaking, and appearing on TV sometimes. I'd never considered how vital my specific language and approach was to connecting with students. Perhaps I was good, but is that good enough when these students face an epidemic?

Reflecting upon my talks, I remembered seeing one-third of the students drifting off during my lectures. I figured that was normal because, yes, they were sleep-deprived and overtasked. Of course, a high percentage would naturally nod off during a talk.

I thought again.

No, I'm not great at reaching students. This principal thinks I'm good because he's comparing me to someone who had half the student body nodding off, not one-third. I think I'm good because my ego is grasping for the compliment. I'm not showing any humility whatsoever in speaking to these students. In fact, I'm not doing the hard work needed to reach them, all of them.

I began studying communication techniques that work with teens. I found considerable resources, all generally offering similar tips like "listen," "don't judge," and "do as I do, not as I say (be a role model)." I paused and thought about the times students did come up to me after talks to engage.

What did they say when they approached me after talks?

Some explained they battled an eating disorder, others marijuana misuse, and others anxiety and depression. Yet each shared a common desire: *joy.*

How do I get to joy and wellbeing? That's what they asked me with their words and their weary eyes.

The following week I made a straightforward adjustment to the "Things Have Changed" talk I frequently deliver to students. I decided to hit the stage with energy, a smile symbolic of joy, and a big welcome.

"Hello, Oxford High School!

"It's such an honor to be here, and, first, I'd like to clear up any confusion. I'm not sure why you think I'm here, but let me tell you why.

"I'm here for one reason, and one reason only. I care so much about you that I want to help you find and keep your joy."

Silence.

But I could see them sitting upright, opening their eyes, looking away from their phones.

"Let me ask, is that something you want? Do you want joy?"

Mild applause.

"Let me ask again," I said, turning up my intensity, "do you want joy that you can have and keep forever? Tell me, do you want joy?"

"Yes!" they shouted back with enthusiastic applause.

Ten minutes into the speech, I was talking about my daughter's eating disorder battle, and I looked into the audience and saw multiple young ladies with tears running down their cheeks. Five minutes later, I was explaining that street marijuana is now 300 to 400 percent higher in THC, the ingredient that makes you high, making it addictive and damaging, and a dozen young men were nodding in accord. And so began the story of how a balding man in his midfifties became a voice and advocate not for the students but with the students, thanks to the slightest adjustments to his speech. Instead of giving them the usual alcohol, drug, and mental health talk, I spoke to them about how to find and keep their joy. I made it about them, not about someone in their parents' or grandparents' generation telling them what they should and shouldn't do.

Substances steal joy, as do mental health problems. And you'll see this theme resonate throughout this book because I've learned it's the golden key to both reaching and saving our students. Parents and educators today must become joy leaders, helping children unlock and keep the joy they want and deserve. More than getting good grades, more than winning a championship—they want sustainable joy. Yet we don't spend much time or effort on helping them see how to achieve that. We're so busy telling them what they need to do, over and over and over again. It's a wonder they don't run away from home and never come back.

Wait, yes, but many do, smoking marijuana or purging the family dinner once out of sight while parents pour themselves an evening glass of wine, basking in a warm glow and considering the day a success.

We assume we know what will give children joy, things like being great at playing the violin or soccer, acing algebra, or swimming faster than the others at lessons—and we shove all that and more at them through high school and into college. Speaking of college, we don't even want them to have a mediocre dormitory room. It's got to be better than the others, because, sure, that will bring them joy, so we help them decorate it to surpass the others but don't understand when they call home crying midway through the first month on campus, feeling lost and lonely.

"Just focus on what you have, dear," we'll say. "You have everything. That great dorm, so many friends."

"But, Mom . . ."

Maybe the decked-out dorm room gives them joy, or not. I

don't know. I'm not criticizing the details and efforts that make life and its experiences fun. Decked-out dorm rooms can be fun. Absolutely. I'm just making a point. It's that I have heard and learned directly from students that the thing they want most out of life is joy—joy that lasts.

Finding joy is the message landing in a sweet spot for teens and college students. How we communicate with students determines whether we effectively reach them or not. And whether we get through to them or not has so much to do with their momentary state of anxiety and depression.

I wish I had understood this better when my children were teenagers. Often when I speak to students and take their questions, one will ask, "If you could go back and do anything differently, what would it be?"

I have the same answer every time: "I'd be a better communicator."

I wanted so much good for my children, and I was so sure that I knew what was good, or would get them to that good, that I frequently told them how they should feel and what they should do. Yet the anecdotal evidence and research shows that's not how children best thrive. My profession was communications—I was a writer—yet with my children, the ones who mattered most in my life, I was too often a one-sided communicator. I learned the hard way that this didn't work. Once we lost our son William to an accidental drug overdose, I changed my communication behavior with my other two children, who were still in college. Instead of telling them what they should do, I asked them what they wanted to do, and listened. Instead of judging their behavior, I modeled my own. And it made all the difference.

Now, I work hard at communicating with students on

their terms, not mine, and it works much better. It's never easy, but I'm always surprised and delighted at the honesty and engaged feedback that comes my way when I deploy good communication tactics. I now understand how critical it is for parents, educators, and all of us who get to engage regularly with students to always use the best communication practices, because they can and will make all the difference. These include:

- Ask open-ended questions.
- Listen, listen, and listen.
- Don't accuse or assume you know.
- Validate children's feelings (they need to be seen and heard).
- Deliver clear and sincere praise (self-esteem matters).
- Engage often over meals and activities (and avoid preaching).
- Don't judge children or others.

JOY MATTERS MOST

It's not so much about happiness for students, though happiness is good, and desired. We want happy students, but no human is happy all the time. We want to strive for something more profound, and lasting. Happiness is fleeting, tied to moments, and doesn't always help anchor one's foundation. Yet that's what we parents seek all too often with our children—happiness and affirmation of it so we feel better in the moment.

We'll even ask them, obsessively, "Are you happy?" Or, "How are you feeling?"

"Yes, sure," they'll say in words, "I'm feeling fine," before adding body language that says, "Can we move on?"

Happiness is a state of mind, or a mood, that often comes from external things or associations. Happiness is so in the moment that it can even double-cross us, making us fear its loss the moment we are experiencing it. Think of watching your team winning a big game. It feels so good, but you can't help think, *Oh no, we play a better team next; I'm afraid we'll lose that game.* Joy, meanwhile, is more profound, less a chased commodity. Joy runs deeper than a feeling that we are good and okay, and it's a key to a sustained and satisfying life. Wellbeing involves it all, including happiness and physical and emotional health, and, yes, A's and championships can be a part of that, too. It's wellbeing we should want for our children. And it's wellbeing that we must help them achieve.

They need help—from parents, educators, and the community—and that help starts here, now. In the pages ahead I'll cover what students today face that threatens their joy, including social media, dangerous and addictive street marijuana, counterfeit prescription pills, fentanyl, and stigma. But we'll also get into the solutions, how active listening, parent role modeling, early counseling, and other strategies can and will make all the difference.

The subject matter may feel heavy at times, or threatening even, because when we effectively, honestly outline what students face in our things-have-changed world, it's enough to scare most of us into a corner of denial. And for many, that's exactly what happens. But they need you, and they need us all to better understand both the problems and solutions, and they need us to better understand how to help them. The healing journey for your child, or the child you get to teach or otherwise mentor and lead, begins here.

TAKEAWAYS

- How we communicate with teens and college students matters.
- Preaching doesn't work as well as teaching.
- They all want joy. We must help them find and keep it.

2

BREAK THE STIGMA

Fear—a strong human emotion that helps us survive—is hard-wired into our brains.

That water is a long way down from the cliff. Don't jump.

The trip is more than we can afford. It's a no go.

Fear saves us. But, like all human strengths, fear also works against us, particularly when what we fear becomes stigmatized.

Stigma is the mark of shame or discredit, and there are few things we parents fear more than our children being associated with shame or discredit. We'll push back against that with substantial fear, even if it means overlooking an obvious problem. Consider a call I got from the parent of a high school senior, one that illustrates, in essence, how almost every call I get from concerned parents of high school and college students goes. The father didn't know me. He'd gotten my number from a mutual friend who knew about my work with young people on substance misuse and mental health issues, and called looking for advice. It was late in the fall semester, and his oldest child, Bill, had all A's, a nearly perfect ACT score, and a starting position on the wrestling team. With his outgoing personality, almost every college and university option imaginable was available.

But Bill's graduation from high school was in doubt despite the accolades. Thus, the father's phone call.

My position in accepting such calls is this: I'm not a counselor and I don't spend even a second attempting to act as one. My goal, always, is to get students (or others) into counseling or treatment. I serve as a lay interventionist of sorts when people reach out for advice—a common first step involving someone facing substance misuse issues. Substance use disorder is a mental health disorder, meaning almost every case requires professional help.

Bill, the father explained, was caught with a handle of vodka on an overnight school trip. The school has a two-strike, no-alcohol policy, and Bill had already been caught once before. For the first offense, Bill had attended a mandatory alcohol and drug awareness class, which included a visit to an open-community Alcoholics Anonymous meeting. He knew that another strike meant school expulsion. The father was initially upset with his son, but the son provided a contextual explanation.

"It's my senior year," he said. "Everybody else was drinking. I just wanted to have some fun."

The school provided a different version of the story. The principal said the school caught several other students with alcohol on the trip, but Bill had the handle of liquor in his room and drank late into the night alone (his trip roommate did not drink). Bill left the half-consumed handle in his room, and the school discovered it on a checkout sweep of all the rooms. "I know my son may not tell me the entire truth," the father said, "but he's usually honest with me. But the school is saying Bill needs to leave for treatment. If he completes a thirty-day residential substance program, he can come back, finish the year, and graduate. Otherwise, he's done."

The father listed reasons he viewed the treatment option as a bad idea. "He'll get labeled as a drunk. Everyone will know. He'll miss winter sports—his last chance to wrestle. It will follow him for the rest of his life. Besides, he's just having fun. He's a senior in high school, and that's what they do."

I asked questions to learn more, like Bill's age when he first got caught drinking or using a substance like marijuana.

"Eighth grade," his father said.

Had Bill gotten into other trouble related to substance misuse? "Yes, well, we went out of town when Bill was in the tenth grade, and he and some friends had a party when they were supposed to be at a friend's house while we were gone. Bill got drunk, threw up all over his bathroom, and blacked out in a corner. His friends called, worried, and we had to send the parents over. But he promised never to do that again, and he hasn't, as far as we know."

Anything else?

"We know he's been using marijuana. But they all do that, right? I mean, it's legal in some states, and he says it helps with his anxiety."

Does he have anxiety? "Yes, it's related to his attention deficit disorder, I think. He's been on Adderall since the eighth grade."

"So he's been on doctor-prescribed Adderall since middle school and has used alcohol and marijuana since then?" I said, framing the situation. "Now, the school suggests he needs substance help, but you think they are wrong?"

"Well, yes," the father said. "I think if he understands that he can't do this again, he'll obey. He's not stupid and is one of the brightest in the entire school, and he's not going to throw away his opportunity for something silly like having fun."

"But isn't that what's just happened?" I said. "Wasn't Bill down to one strike? Yet he went on a school trip with a handle of vodka and drank it alone in his room late at night. I must say, this behavior suggests that Bill has a substance use disorder. Treatment is what he needs. It's too big for you to try to fix by punishing him and asking him to make a promise that he likely can't keep."

The father was momentarily silent.

"Hello?" I asked.

"Look," he said, "Bill is just having fun, like all the seniors. I don't think he's got a problem. But he will if he gets labeled as a drunk."

It was the middle of the pandemic, and the father concluded that finishing high school remotely was a better option than leaving for treatment. I wanted to reiterate to him that there was no shame in what his son was facing—statistics show that at least one in every five children experience a mental health disorder, and that at least half don't get the help they need, deepening the problem. Instead, I stopped the information train, figuring his mind was made up, for now.

"Good luck," I said. "Keep me posted."

DON'T POSTPONE NEEDED HELP

A year later, I received a text message from Bill's father. "Can you talk?" he asked.

We got on the phone, and the father said Bill had finished high school at home and couldn't participate in graduation ceremonies, but he'd had no obvious substance issues and had headed off to an Ivy League university, according to plan. That started okay, the father said. Bill pledged a fraternity, made numerous friends, and enjoyed the college social scene. At the midterm, Bill had all A's. There had been a scare. The father had gotten a call from the local hospital emergency room in early October. Bill had fainted walking to lunch after a long party night. He was diagnosed with dehydration and exhaustion, and Bill told his father he'd been pushing too hard, trying to keep up with his peers' partying and studying, but he promised to do better and slow down.

The father said finals were about to start and the semester was almost complete, but Bill had called home the night before, sounding an alarm.

"My son said he needs help," the father said. "Substance help, I think. He said he's struggling with anxiety and alcohol and needs help. I'm trying to talk him into finishing exams, coming home, and then getting an appointment to see his psychiatrist and figure out what's going on, but my wife said I should call you to think through the best plan."

"Ah, well, I'm glad you called," I told the father. "Let me start by sharing one of the late Maya Angelou's favorite sayings: 'People know themselves much better than you do.' So, if someone says they are crazy, believe them. If someone says they need help, believe them. Bill gave you an SOS call, and I suggest we find him a treatment center for enrollment by the end of today or early tomorrow. He can likely get an extension on his exams for the health emergency and get the help he needs without academic issues."

"I guess you're right," the father said. "I've just been so afraid, wanting Bill to have everything he's worked for."

"He can still have that and more," I said. "Once he finds his true self and stands on a strong foundation of personal confidence and strength. And when he does, that's how he'll be seen and labeled."

The father kept me updated as Bill finished one treatment and then enrolled in another before moving into sober housing and settling into a new metro area. Along the journey, Bill increasingly revealed details to his family about his substance misuse. He'd been using cocaine and Xanax without a prescription since high school. He had been drinking a couple of handles of vodka a week since high school and using marijuana daily.

"He says he's an addict," Bill's father said. "He says he's suffered from the disease since middle school or early high school, but he's doing something about it now. And he sounds great, he does, and I've never heard him speak from such a place of peace and self-confidence."

I'd never heard the father speak about his son with such peace or confidence either. His fear of any labeling his son might face was gone.

"We should have encouraged him to deal with this sooner," the father said.

"Don't beat yourself up," I said. "I made the same mistake with my sons. We can only hope to learn along the way and share that wisdom with others. Also, it's not just you or me. The entire student ecosystem can work against those suffering."

"What do you mean?"

"I mean, look at the school," I said. "Bill was suffering from substance use disorder, defined by health experts as a disease affecting the brain and behavior around substances including alcohol and marijuana. The key word is *disease*."

"Okay, I'm listening," the father said.

"If Bill had had cancer in high school, that school would

have expressed sympathy for his suffering from the disease and worked overtime to accommodate him through graduation. But because Bill's disease of substance use disorder has a stigma, the school wanted no part of it, due to the school's fear of stigma. The principal said Bill could leave the school and get help, with the opportunity to return upon completion of treatment, or leave the school for good if he didn't, and those were the options given for Bill's disease. I was hoping for local outpatient treatment while he remained in school."

"It's messed up," the father said.

"That's an understatement."

WAYS OF BREAKING THE STIGMA

We don't have to be ruled by stigma. There are key ways that we can break some of the common narratives surrounding mental health and substance misuse to empower our children and ourselves to overcome our fears and instead seek solutions.

- Share real-life examples of people coping with mental health or substance use disorder to put a face on it.
- Let children know that substance use disorder is a treatable disease, not a personal weakness.
- Avoid talking in judgmental tones or words about anyone who suffers a mental health or substance use disorder.
- Try not to frame your child's life sequence for

them; if you do, your child might fear letting you down if circumstances suggest they need change.

- If you've received counseling or struggled, share that experience with your child if and when appropriate.
- Don't judge the behavior or struggles of your children's peers. Use them as educational discussion points related to your child.

WHAT SCHOOLS FACE

Schools face stigma around substance misuse just as students and families do, and that's one reason why Bill and his son had a difficult time navigating their situation. There's no established, clear path for handling a substance misuse issue involving a teen or college student. Parents aren't sure what to do, and educators don't always have the best solution for the student. They have what appears to be the best solution for the school and its reputation—separation from the problem.

Truthfully, many schools fear the label; they don't want someone calling their institution a "drug school." We've all heard such talk—"[named school] has a drug problem"—and while this kind of thinking is misinformed and misplaced, it repeatedly happens. Schools can't have a drug problem, though. Schools are merely collections of students from families within the community. Substance issues are family and community problems that show up in our schools, colleges, and universities. Still, some schools have feared such labeling to the point that they don't offer the needed education about substance misuse. In recent years, however, the mental health and substance use crisis has escalated to the point that many schools feel they can no longer ignore it. It's just that agreeing upon a solution for educating and leading students around behavioral health is challenging for several reasons beyond the obvious—schools were not created with a primary mission of delivering holistic education. The current political environment makes anything introduced beyond introductory courses hard for schools, which is ironic since we know that the bitter, biting politics that clogs up the news cycle has contributed negatively to youth mental health.

"I can't sleep," said a sixteen-year-old in 2018, according to a University of Michigan survey.

"I'm scared for my safety," said a fifteen-year-old in the same survey, sharing how politics directly affected student wellbeing.

Schools get caught in the crosshairs of political stress, which was elevated during the COVID-19 pandemic due to disagreements over masks, vaccines, testing policies, and whether to provide in-person classes or remote learning. According to one study, nearly 41 percent of teachers considered quitting or retiring during the 2020–2021 school year because the environment was too taxing. At the same time, student mental health deteriorated, according to agencies like the U.S. Centers for Disease Control and Prevention (CDC). School administrators and teachers were drowning in both new COVID-19 policies and student and parental blowback that teaching traditional classes like science and executing extracurricular activities was challenging enough. Creating and introducing a new behavioral health curriculum felt impossible.

COVID-19 wasn't the only obstacle. The political

environment in this country has deteriorated in the past decade to the point that many schools have become conflict shy, making the introduction of substance curriculum uncomfortable. Also, school programs in the past didn't work so well. Just Say No, the well-known antidrug campaign that former American First Lady Nancy Reagan started in 1982, encouraged students to "just say no" if offered alcohol and other drugs. And while it wasn't a school program, the First Lady's attention to the issue amid America's highly publicized increase in crack cocaine usage created an urgency among parents and educators. When the Los Angeles police chief began a new program called DARE (Drug Abuse Resistance Education), federal funding was available and schools readily accepted the program. DARE spread to more than 75 percent of American schools, but there was just one problem—it had no beneficial statistical outcomes. That's right, no positive results. America poured hundreds of millions of dollars into a program that wasn't backed by positive research outcomes, that involved authority figures in uniform telling youth what they should not do, and that likely only created stigma, reinforcing to elementary school students that chronic drug users are criminals rather than individuals battling a disease.

In addition to examining the content of these programs, consider that adults delivered DARE's and Just Say No's messaging to students when studies show it is peer-led mental health and substance misuse education that works best. Go figure. That's why I've been working in my day job with others in the William Magee Institute for Student Wellbeing at the University of Mississippi on developing peer-to-peer education teams to address middle school and high school students. We don't call them alcohol and drug awareness teams either. They are happiness teams because almost every student wants happiness and joy, but they don't want someone giving them a "drug talk." Not at all.

We train student engagement team members to connect with students in a relatable manner and help their peers understand how substances steal joy. Almost all students want happiness, and they'll listen to strategies for getting there from fellow students. Team members are trained in delivery and in telling their stories with authenticity, with details of challenges faced and overcome, in order to break the stigma and deliver hope.

We began the program because schools asked for additional help during many of my speaking visits. There's just one of me, but more importantly, I'm in my late fifties, with deep, well-earned lines of experience and a graying, receding hairline. Sure, I can engage with students, but shouldn't I focus more on parents, sending a team of peer-to-peer educators to connect and engage with students more deeply? Exactly.

The strategy makes sense because, as mentioned, research clearly shows that students respond best to peer-to-peer education. Also, there's a wise saying that "students get students on drugs, and students can get students off drugs" (or keep them from starting in the first place). Yet do a quick scan throughout your community to find the peer-to-peer programs—some exist but not many—and you'll find that those that do exist have messaging and approaches that are not developed enough for full impact. And odds are high that you won't find one in your community or nearby at all. The odds are also high that your community and the surrounding ones have a high percentage of students in grades 6–12 and college struggling with mental health, substance misuse, or both. Now, imagine if each of those students, beginning in the sixth grade, received repeated engagement with teams of storytelling peers who shared personal experiences and clearly stated facts related to how those students can find and keep joy. By breaking the stigma upstream and reaching youth earlier, we turn the tide of the epidemic today and tomorrow, as those students will be better-prepared parents and mentors one day.

That's why many schools and educators are joining us on this mission to find and implement new and better solutions—solutions that align honestly with the problem and directly with the best-outcomes approach, which involves communicating with students on their terms.

It's not just schools that need peer education programs either. Consider churches, long leaders in family and teen education. Yes, church membership remains in steady decline across America. Yet most teens still identify as religious, and more than 70 percent attend religious services periodically, according to a 2020 Pew Research Center report. That means churches and church youth groups are in the ecosystem of many students, presenting more opportunities for mental health and substance misuse education. It's not a far reach for churches, considering that when divorce rates skyrocketed in the 1970s, churches throughout America recognized their core unit was at risk and implemented marriage education as a foundational aspect of ministry. They've not yet been quick to act on the student mental health and substance misuse crisis, but I hope that will change soon. When I've had that discussion with pastors, they've responded affirmatively, as if it's an altogether new concept that makes so much sense. Digging in, however, is something different because it's a complicated, heavy subject matter for the church. Talking about techniques to strengthen marriage among adults in the church is one thing, while discussing illegal marijuana, prescription pills, or fentanyl with teens in the church is quite another thing. Some parents might blame the church for exposing their children to drugs, for instance, especially if straight-talking peers connect with the youth. That's why this movement of turning back the epidemic must start with parents.

We parents want so much good for our children. So it might seem that getting parents up-to-date on this crisis and engaged in action would be easy, but it's not. Sure, most will get emotional and engage in conversation whenever drugs come up regarding their children or peers. The scenario typically starts like it did for Bill and his father, however. The desire is there, but stigma gets in the way on multiple levels. If we are honest, we in this country still see drug users as lower-class citizens. The facts speak otherwise, but if I say the words "drug dealer" to a parent, they'll admit to picturing some shady character standing on a street corner peddling illegal substances. They don't see their child, whose been caught selling such substances to friends, as a drug dealer.

If I say the word "addict" to a parent (this term isn't favored by health care providers, but sometimes it's helpful in making a point), they'll imagine a frail, scabby, toothless person on a street corner. They won't see their son or daughter who's selling the family silver to buy counterfeit Adderall. Many believe impoverished neighborhoods are "drug ridden" while their upper-middle-class suburbia is merely battling "anxiety" with its drugs. Never mind that research has shown that upper-middle-class individuals are two to three times more likely to suffer from substance use disorder by age twenty-six than individuals nationally. It's not that they are bad people. Not at all. But stigma prevents us from seeing the truth.

The crisis that students, and therefore families, face today is not limited to any geography, sex, race, or economy. It's just that many parents, like Bill's father, fear the stigma more than facing that reality. They'll admit their uncle had a drinking problem, and perhaps their mother, too. But they will reject the notion that their child may struggle with substances, even though studies show that the younger generation's time from initial use to full-blown substance use disorder can be so much shorter. Parents want to set their child on a pedestal above the others not because of love but because of fear.

BRING DOWN THE WALL

Bill's father loved him so much and wanted him to have the best, as long as that didn't require saying he suffered from addiction, because Bill's father feared this acknowledgment would lower Bill's standing in the world and limit his opportunities.

I'm not judging the father, or any other parents with similar views, because I have been that parent. I have made the same mistake—regarding myself, regarding my children. When I spiraled into substance misuse, losing my marriage and career (before gaining them both back better than before in sobriety), I didn't think I had a problem because I could look around and find friends and others who drank more than me. I saw and cited examples all around me that normalized my behavior. I thought an addict could not quit without experiencing difficult withdrawal symptoms.

"I'm not addicted to anything," I said, considering physical withdrawal as the only sign of addiction. Not until I looked beyond physical addiction to addiction's consequences—divorce, professional failure, financial peril, physical health—did I take myself off the pedestal. Finally, I recognized that I was no different from the addicts I had pictured in my mind whose lives looked so different from the one I was living.

The reality was just as hard with my children because I didn't want to see the truth for fear of how the world might perceive them. My son William was all-state in track and field in high school, spoke Spanish fluently, was active in a church youth group, and had a vibrant social life. But the signs of a problem were abundant. My wife and I found a crude, home-made marijuana bong in his closet when he was in the ninth grade. "Just experimenting," he said. He dinged his car on a Friday night with friends in the tenth grade. "Someone parked too close to me," he said. He got caught drinking on a school trip. "Everyone was doing it," he explained. And on and on this went into college with increasing peril until his senior year, when substance use disorder became obvious. But even then, even understanding that he suffered from a disease, we battled stigma.

"You need help," we told William.

"Maybe," he said. "But it's my senior year, and I need to graduate and finish my honors college thesis."

The signs of struggle said he needed immediate help at the finish line of college. But his friends, including his girlfriend, were graduating. Maybe he had a point. Just two more months, then he'd be done—a graduate like the rest. No stigma attached.

William did graduate from the University of Mississippi, though he never finished his honors college thesis. He couldn't concentrate enough on that.

"I went too far," he told me. "I can't focus enough anymore."

He got his diploma, and in our parental picture, that was

something. And he got into treatment a couple of months later as hoped. It became clearer, however, how significantly he suffered from substance use disorder. William got kicked out of one treatment center because he managed to buy a bottle of cough syrup and drank it to get high. He got kicked out of another because he and another client figured out how to get one fentanyl pill each and got caught when their glassy eyes were a giveaway to the counselor. Eventually, after five or six thirty-day stays at various treatment centers—which seemed extreme, though I learned that's quite normal—he found his pace in sobriety for several months before relapsing. Ultimately, I found him dead from an overdose, and I wished I could take back the many years we did not deal with his obvious problem, just because we didn't want him labeled or set on a different path from his peers. Seeing the devastating consequences of bowing to stigma made me realize that stigmatizing these issues is one of the most significant barriers to supporting our children's behavioral health. Previously, I saw *behavioral health* as some vague term I didn't understand, something that academics used. But after William's death, I understood how much more important caring for behavioral health is than worrying about stigma. The signs showed up early in high school. William had a disease and needed help. By the time he got into treatment at the age of twenty-two, he was regularly abusing alcohol, cocaine, marijuana, and opiates, and his brain was so deeply affected that the journey back was much harder than it would have been had he gotten help sooner.

That's why months later, when our daughter, Mary Halley, a college freshman, explained she was suffering from an eating disorder, purging and controlling intake, we didn't hesitate to take action and worked with her to find help and make the changes she needed. She said she wanted to transfer universities, and while we initially thought about the stigma that might incur, we relented. Mary Halley also began seeing a counselor and working with a nutritionist. She even did horse therapy, something we didn't initially understand and didn't quite have the money for but we managed. Mary Halley is now years into eating disorder recovery and a mother of three. Grandchildren are among our greatest joys. I have no doubt that had we talked Mary Halley into staying at the university where she began (in order to keep our picture of her college life intact), instead of relenting on the transfer and doubling down on aggressive eating disorder treatment, we wouldn't have that joy nor would she.

We now understand the value of early care when the signs are there. We know stigma is a wall that parents must figure out how to knock down for the love of children who need help. They need you to help break the stigma, and also to see beyond it. Their wellbeing depends on it.

TAKEAWAYS

- Parents want what's best for their children, but fear can cause delays or avoidance of counseling and treatment.
- Schools face stigma, too, but holistic education is needed.
- It's not about what the parent (or educator) wants. It's about what the child deserves.

3

THE SMARTPHONE AND SOCIAL MEDIA DILEMMA

When Kade Webb, twenty, was found dead in the bathroom of a Safeway Market in Roseville, California, in 2022, police opened his smartphone and social media apps to search for clues about his cause of death. They found exactly what they expected—evidence of a drug purchase of a supposed prescription pill that was actually a counterfeit pill laced with fentanyl.

"Mr. Webb, a laid-back snowboarder and skateboarder who, with the imminent birth of his first child, had become despondent over his pandemic-dimmed finances, bought Percocet, a prescription opioid, through a dealer on Snapchat," reported the *New York Times*. "It turned out to be spiked with a lethal amount of fentanyl."

Such overdose deaths of young Americans rose at an alarming rate in 2021 and 2022, with more than 108,000 in 2021 alone, according to the CDC. But just as shocking as the deaths is the fact that smartphones and associated social media apps have become the mode of standard operation for purchasing illegal drugs.

We should have seen this coming; today's students are the first generation to have their lives shaped by next-generation smartphones and associated apps. Think about it. Apple's iPhone did not release until 2007, and the social media app Instagram didn't launch until 2010, with Snapchat following in 2011. Now these apps and others are among the primary tools teenagers and college students use to buy and sell drugs. It's hard to imagine that's what technology developers had in mind when creating these products, but that's the reality of how they've come to be used.

Venmo? The app launched in 2009 and was aimed at family and friends who wanted to split bills for dinner, movies, or a night at the bar or bowling alley. It and other cash exchange apps like Zelle, Cash App, and Remitly do all that and more, and frequently I'll ask unsuspecting parents if their child is into illegal drugs and if they've checked their child's Venmo account. Yes, they usually say to the latter question, and?

I smile, waiting.

And?

"You think all that activity in a day is your son splitting food bills with friends? How many times can he eat in a day? Kids have emoji codes as a language among themselves. Fifteen different food transactions in a day among friends is not likely food, and they are probably selling weed or other illegal substances to friends."

Even deadly fentanyl, created as a powerful painkiller for late-stage cancer patients, is sold to teens primarily through social media, with cash payments cleared on Venmo and similar apps.

It's no accident that this chapter on smartphones is near the front of the book and follows the chapter about stigma. This advanced device, a high-powered, portable personal computer, and its associated apps have more to do with the mental health and substance misuse epidemic than most parents and educators can conceive. If given a choice, most educators would ban smartphones from schools, but these devices have become such a big part of students' lives, including how students and their families stay connected, that there's not much schools can do. One high school teacher told me that the faculty knows that if a student's eyes aren't focused on the front of the classroom, odds are high that they are stealing glances at their phone, but teachers' hands are tied. "We've been down that road [of trying to take phones away]. It didn't fly."

The distractions smartphones and apps cause in teen lives are known, but recognizing a challenge and doing something about it are two different things, since many teens view the smartphone as necessary to life, as essential as the air they breathe. The apps tether users to their devices through addictive qualities, which lead to more unhealthy thoughts, feelings, and behavior, and it's getting worse by the minute. Consider that in 2015, 32 percent of American eleven-year-olds owned a smartphone, and by 2019 that number had increased to 53 percent, according to a Common Sense Media survey. Teens rack up more than seven hours daily of screen time, not counting time for homework or school, but that fact alone is perhaps not problematic. The trouble is that smartphones and associated apps are linked to early accidental pornography viewing by children, sleep disturbance, illegal substance pushing and purchasing among teens, and eating disorders and other mental health issues. There's no shortage of studies in the smartphone era suggesting a link between screen time and a decline in mental health, but some experts question that conclusion.

"Why else might American kids be anxious other than telephones?" Jeff Hancock, founder of the Stanford Social Media Lab, told the *New York Times*. "How about climate change? How about income inequality? How about more student debt? There are so many big giant structural issues that have a huge impact on us but are invisible and that we aren't looking at."

Stanford's Hancock makes a valid point—it's not the phone itself, or the time spent staring at its screen. Suppose students spent seven hours on their devices daily, dividing time between streaming Discovery Channel shows and reading the *Wall Street Journal* and the *New York Times*. In that case, they might be concerned about world issues but also well-informed, and they might not develop body image issues or suffer from depression. It rarely works that way, though. Most students don't consume news anymore. A study published by the American Psychological Association in 2018 revealed that "less than 20 percent of U.S. teens report reading a book, magazine or daily newspaper for pleasure while more than 80 percent use social media every day."

Many teens do consume pornography on their smartphones, however. Teens may initially find it accidentally, but some studies show they are among the most significant consumers of online porn in America. Also, smartphones and associated apps have become primary tools for purchasing drugs. For example, the father of a college student who died of an accidental fentanyl overdose told me that after his son's death he spent hours looking in his son's smartphone. He searched for clues about what went wrong and found an endless stream of drug-pushing social media messages targeting his son. That's because algorithms are used on social media, and even a few explorations of illegal drug content on TikTok or Instagram can unlock a barrage. It's not that the algorithms directly tell pushers which social users are surfing the content so they can then message. Rather, those searching for or even glancing at drug-related content show up in recommended follows to the pushers, thanks to the algorithm, and the pushers send chats in response. It's not what these kids asked for, but that's how social media takes advantage of users—one's curiosity can gain unintended momentum.

I've told students I feel like my generation owes them an apology, and I'll apologize. "I'm sorry. We've let you down, handing you devices that provide a gateway to your weak spots."

In my youth, I learned early on in high school that alcohol was not my friend. I passed out on a date night from too much vodka, and my grades suffered. But I feared illegal drugs and avoided them. I imagine, however, that if I'd had a smartphone and spent seven hours or more a day surfing social media, using applications that were gateways for dozens of daily messages promising me all kinds of joy through pills and other substances, I would not have been able to resist. All that's required is one short response, and boom! Home delivery via DoorDash. Yes, that's right, DoorDash. It works like this: the drug dealer and prospective client exchange messages on platforms like WhatsApp or Snapchat.

"4 percs, 2 Add," the buyer might say, meaning they want four (counterfeit) Percocet pills and two (counterfeit) Adderall pills.

"Make a food order through [restaurant name] and I'll bring them over," the drug dealer might say.

Ding-dong, your food delivery has arrived—and here are your pills.

As a high schooler, might I have made a purchase? Yes.

Might I have kept purchasing again and again once I got, say, a few counterfeit Adderall pills laced with fentanyl fired into my dopamine receptors? Undoubtedly.

Might it have killed me by the age of sixteen? Likely.

Students these days are proverbial sitting ducks on smartphones because most of today's teens began using the popular apps in middle school or earlier.

THE EATING DISORDER LINK

Consider that the marketing and purchasing of illegal drugs aren't the only problems teens face with smartphones and social media apps. Increasingly, studies show links between some social media apps and mental health issues, including eating disorders, which have risen rapidly, particularly among adolescent girls. Apps like Instagram, which feature filters for changing appearances and showcase so many curated images, can distort reality.

"There is no single cause of body dissatisfaction or disordered eating," reports the National Eating Disorders Association. "However, research is increasingly clear that media does indeed contribute and that exposure to and pressure exerted by media increase body dissatisfaction and disordered eating."

In my extended family, several people battle or have battled eating disorders and body image issues. Each can talk for hours about triggers and negative feelings they get from social media. They'll go through periods of swearing off social media but return eventually despite the pain. It's also safe to say that every female in my extended family has expressed significant anxiety related to social media, Instagram in particular, at one point or another. That's not to suggest it's a female-only issue. Of course not. But there's no denying that females suffer more. Studies reveal this is true, and I know it anecdotally because I talk to many college students, male and female, often several hundred or more at a time.

It's become routine for multiple female students to express negative feelings about social media issues in discussions after my talk, while it comes up less frequently for male students. Statistics confirm my perceptions, indicating that two out of three individuals, or roughly 66 percent, suffering from an eating disorder in the United States are female. Still, that leaves 33 percent—a substantial number—of males suffering from an eating disorder. So we must be careful not to label it as a girls-only condition, because that's untrue. For young males, an eating disorder can be harder to detect, because although it might involve getting too thin, it's frequently about achieving a "perfect sculpted body." The Child Mind Institute calls this manifestation "reverse anorexia" or "bigorexia."

"These boys have all the psychological features of anorexia, except they're pushing it in the opposite direction," according to Douglas Bunnell, PhD, a child psychologist and expert on eating disorders.

Signs of male eating disorders include eating large amounts of food, exercising excessively, refusing certain food groups, and constantly weighing oneself and looking in the mirror.

In fact, eating disorders among young men are among the fastest-growing problems I see in the collegiate population, and frequently these students experience significant shame, due to the stigma that it's a female problem. I learned this firsthand from a young man who reached out looking for a counseling referral. Tom was a rising sophomore at Auburn University, and his father had read my book *Dear William* and learned about the William Magee Center at the University of Mississippi. Tom's father assumed, rightly, that I might know the best first steps for battling his eating disorder, and he connected us.

"I hope you'll keep this confidential," said Tom (not his real name).

"Of course," I said. "I get to talk to lots of students from all over the country. It's all confidential unless there is in immediate threat to their life."

"Okay," Tom said, "but I mean I can't have anyone know this."

"Know what? Tell me what's going on, and I'll point you in the right direction for help immediately."

"Well," he explained, "I'm binge eating. A lot. I'll leave a party to do it. I'll stay up late and do it. I just eat everything I can get my hands on and then I feel sick."

"Do you purge?"

"No. I don't purge," Tom explained. "But I fast for the next several days so I don't gain weight."

"How do you handle that as a college student?"

"I haven't let my grades go down. I've got all A's. I get

grumpy, though. My parents say they can't talk to me when I'm fasting and I don't feel like being with friends."

Tom told me he'd played football in high school and was All-Conference. He'd had the chance to play small-college football but opted for fraternity life at a Southeastern Conference school instead. "My friends don't know about my eating disorder," he said, "but they know something is going on."

He said he was active in church in the college town and held a fraternity office, as chaplain.

"I look good on paper, I guess, like I have it all together. But I'm struggling, really struggling."

"Listen, Tom," I said. "Everybody struggles. You are not alone. I'll give you the name of a counselor to call in the next few minutes."

Girls can also hide their eating disorder in plain sight, suffering while nobody notices.

I've known multiple female students who were suffering from an eating disorder but were not underweight. Some have even said their parents don't take them seriously because of preconceived notions of what people with an eating disorder should look like. These girls sounded almost insulted, as if they were thinking, *I'm doing this damaging behavior and you don't believe me?*

One young woman approached me at her high school after I gave a talk, and she explained how her situation had transpired. "I started purging in middle school," she explained. "I didn't lose weight, but my mother noticed [residue] around the toilet. She talked to me like I was stupid. 'You are losing good meals for nothing.' I had a friend taking lots of laxatives daily so I started doing that. Within three months I'd lose twenty-five pounds and the school nurse called me in. My mother hadn't yet noticed.

"The nurse called my mother in for a talk and my dad came also, and they decided to send me off to treatment. It was spring of ninth grade, and treatment helped and I was back in school for tenth grade."

"What grade are you in now?" I asked.

"I'm a senior," she said. "I want to go to school for counseling and help others."

She told me she'd already spoken at her high school, telling her story to peers. "They all already knew, anyway," she said, smiling. "I just supplied the details for the story they'd already heard."

My daughter, Mary Halley, was in high school when her eating disorder began, which is not uncommon. Hers didn't start via social media, but social media undoubtedly contributed. Initially, the trigger was related to a boyfriend and the bullying that coincided with the start of their relationship. Friends of the boyfriend's ex, who were also my daughter's friends, initially iced her at school and after-school social events. Soon, that passive-aggressive response intensified into name-calling and accusations through social media messaging that the boyfriend was stealing. It all transpired amid a crisis at home—I was struggling with substance misuse, and so were my sons, and my marriage was at risk. Studies show that this type of at-home stress greatly increases the odds of student mental health issues, and my daughter was no different from the others who succumbed. Social media fanned the flames. Her food consumption increased. She gained weight. When logging onto social media, she faced harsh messages and images of friends posing with one another, supposedly having the time of their lives, while she was left out. The more she looked at the imagery, the more she saw inadequacy in her weight as compared to the perfection she saw in their curated images. She began purging.

The stress intensified in our home. My wife and I argued until I moved out. Once I was out, my wife's appetite dwindled, and with our boys away at college, it was just her and our daughter together for dinner. My wife was running her business and exercising daily with yoga to alleviate stress. For dinner, she'd make a baked potato with sautéed spinach. An active senior in high school, Mary Halley was often hungry after dinner and would eat the few available options, like a box of vanilla wafers, which would result in more shame and purging. She'd attempt to remain off social media, which helped in part but also stoked anxiety because it left her out of the loop of peer activity during a period of time that's often billed as one of the most memorable of one's life. She didn't tell her mother or me that she'd developed an eating disorder. Instead, she told a school counselor, who called her mother in for a meeting.

"Mary Halley is purging," the counselor explained. "She needs counseling."

Within a week she saw a nutritionist, a critical defense in battling an eating disorder. We did not, however, align an all-out treatment assault for Mary Halley because the condition was new to us. We didn't understand either the severity of the problem or the aggressive measures required early on to get it under control. Meanwhile, our family life was chaotic and stressful, to say the least. My wife and I divorced, and I temporarily moved across the country. I got my addiction under control, and my wife and I started talking again, but

Mary Halley's brother Hudson nearly died from an accidental drug overdose. He recovered, and one year later her oldest brother, William, died of an accidental drug overdose. Amid that turmoil, as we learned the importance of treatment for substance use disorder, Mary Halley approached us. Seeing Hudson's impressive recovery, she spoke with uncharacteristic intensity.

"I need y'all to hear me," she said. "I'm struggling, really, really struggling. I need help. I need real help."

For the first time, we got it—really got it. Eating disorder carries the same loss of joy and life-and-death seriousness as substance use disorder. Like substance use disorder, eating disorder is so intense that the person suffering can't easily decide to stop. Counseling is required, likely for the long term. A nutritionist is usually also needed, as well as coordination with one's primary care physician. Those undergoing eating disorder treatment need understanding from family regarding their triggers and the type of support required. Yes, it takes a village.

With Mary Halley, this team effort worked. Not quickly, no. But it worked, and over several years she developed a toolbox and a psychological depth of understanding of what she was doing and why to push back against it. Success looks like this: these days, Mary Halley is a married mother of three precious toddlers. On her first day of counseling, she recalls the therapist asking if she wanted children.

"Yes!" my daughter said. "More than anything."

"Well, this disease may not allow that if you don't get it under control."

And on that day, Mary Halley began an earnest fight.

Years later, she says that social media still presents an

obstacle to her joy. She'll log on one day, post a photo of her children, spend a few days periodically visiting an app until she realizes negative thoughts have crept back, and then she'll back off usage again. It's a simple strategy—managing app time to limit triggers—but it's also easier said than done. Mary Halley is now in her late twenties, and years of introspective, successful counseling have helped her develop her toolbox.

DO THEY NEED SMARTPHONES?

Smartphones and associated apps can damage teens even if they aren't getting illegal drug solicitations or experiencing eating disorder triggers. Through sheer distraction—teens spend more than seven hours a day on a device on average—teens today miss out on key interpersonal engagements and learning opportunities. We know, for example, that children develop best with frequent and meaningful engagement with family.

Smartphones and associated apps steal that time. For teens, the world is going by without their notice. We've all experienced it—sitting with teens for dinner while they continuously check apps and messages. Adults distractedly do this as well, and that's worth noting, since, as we'll discuss in chapter nine, the apple does not fall far from the tree. A study by Common Sense Media revealed that four in ten children worry that their parents are addicted to their devices, while seven in ten parents think their children spend too much time on smartphones. Many apps they are using, like Instagram, weren't designed for children and have been shown to be harmful, yet their usage of these apps is increasing fast.

We know that helping teens with restrictions around smartphones and apps can help limit risk. However, parents are easily overwhelmed by the battle to limit smartphone use. It's hard, because once teens have a phone, it's in their hands at all times.

Smartphones reach children at increasingly young ages with the best intentions—safety, security, and education are primary reasons for purchase. And these reasons are valid. We don't need research to know that a teen with a smartphone is reachable at most times and that they can reach us. Many parents track their teens via the GPS on their phones and closely monitor activity. Teens can do homework on smartphones and find easy access to education resources, and most parents believe these benefits make the devices necessary.

Besides, everyone else has one.

Who wants their twelve-year-old child to be the only one in school without a smartphone? They'd be labeled. They'd be out of touch. They'd suffer.

Or would they?

Many notable tech CEOs or company leaders have made news in recent years by wholly or significantly restricting their children's smartphone or tablet access due to perceived risks. The practice began with the late Apple founder and CEO Steve Jobs, who told the *New York Times* before his death that he and his wife limited technology use at home for their children. Instead, they held family dinners together at a big table, discussing books and history.

Another long-time tech executive, Athena Chavarria, who worked as an executive assistant at Facebook, didn't allow her children to have smartphones until they were in high school. Even then she severely limited their usage time because, as

Chavarria told the *New York Times*, she was "convinced the devil lives in our phones and is wreaking havoc on our children."

The nonprofit organization Wait Until 8th operates under the premise that there "is a reason why top Silicon Valley executives are saying no to the smartphone until at least 14 for their children." The organization urges parents to wait until children are in the eighth grade before giving them a smartphone. It lists reasons for delaying, including that smartphones are changing childhood; are addictive; impair sleep; interfere with relationships; increase risk for anxiety, depression, and cyberbullying; and are an academic distraction.

High school teacher Tyler Rablin of Sunnyside, Washington, has seen enough in his experience to conclude that smartphones in the classroom harm children.

The following is a collection of tweets Rablin shared on the subject:

I use to be on the team that's like, "Let kids bring phones into the classroom! We'll use them for learning!" The problem, and the reason I've changed my stance, is simply that the attention economy makes this nearly impossible. It's a losing battle for kids & their brain.

When a student picks up their phone, they are immediately bombarded with notifications and noise, arguably none of which is relevant to their learning. The things that would benefit their learning are not actively reaching out for their attention and time; the things that . . . are noise and distraction are designed to manipulate their brain to get their attention. The phone is no longer a passive tool. Their phone is actively and intentionally working against the goals of learning, of having a productive and meaning-ful life.

Are there creative tools and apps that are beneficial to learning? Yes, absolutely. But I'm not going to take an alcoholic, throw him into a bar, and ask him to only drink the water. I feel like that's what we're doing to kids with their phones in the classroom. It's not even just about the learning. If you look at nearly any study that analyzes the relationship between phone use/notification/social media and mental health, it's virtually always a net negative. Why would I want to allow that to happen in my classroom?

SLEEP DEPRIVED

Slowly but certainly, some researchers studying student behavior and success have recognized that sleep deprivation is affecting nearly nine out of ten students in America. Sleep deprivation is associated with mental health issues, including anxiety, depression, and suicidal thoughts. There's also a clear association between alcohol and marijuana use and sleep deprivation, according to a University of Buffalo study. That's hardly a secret to adults, who know what a few too many glasses of wine at a party do to a person. The next day, you feel sluggish and can't concentrate due to poor sleep quality, regardless of the number of hours spent in bed. It's also known that those with substance misuse tendencies use more when they are tired, so sleep deprivation and substance use feed off each other.

Multiple factors contribute to the student sleep deprivation crisis, according to a Stanford University poll, which indicated that 87 percent of U.S. high school students get less than the recommended eight to ten hours of sleep each night. Specifically, changing social and cultural factors meet fast-changing technology to result in trouble for teens. In fact, Stanford reported in 2015 that "since the early 1990s, it's been established that teens have a biologic tendency to go to sleep later—as much as two hours later—than their younger counterparts."

One high school student, a junior, told me that she was in a serious relationship with her first boyfriend and that it had rewards but also brought anxiety because she worried he'd lose interest. At the same time, her friends were showing less interest in her. She attempted to control anxiety on both sides of this problem by sleeping with her smartphone so she could stay abreast of any messages or posts.

"If my friends share or message me, I feel like I need to respond immediately to stay on their radar," she explained. "Same with my boyfriend. But that leaves me tired and exhausted every day and I feel like I need a long nap. It's harder to concentrate in class and I'm grumpy sometimes with my parents and younger brother."

There's nothing unusual about this story. Stories like it have become the norm. When I speak to students in schools, from middle school to high school and through college, I directly address the risk of smartphones and apps and typically see multiple heads nodding in accord. And I have yet to have one out of thousands deliver anything in response but affirmation.

"Yes," a student told me, "we are the first generation born as prisoners of this device, but what can we do about it?"

More than one-third of all teens get only five to six hours

of sleep a night, according to a 2010 study in the *Journal of Adolescent Health*, while the optimal sleep amount for teens is 9.25 hours nightly. Sleep is being stolen from teens by a perfect storm of interruption, made up of hormones, homework and academic demands, peer pressure, and distractions from their devices. The Child Mind Institute reports:

> It's not just that Facebook, Twitter, Instagram, Tumblr and YouTube are distractions that keep kids up later, it's the actual light coming off the electronic devices they're exposed to, especially late at night. Electronics emit a glow called blue light that has a particular frequency. "When it hits receptors in the eye," says Dr. [Max] Van Gilder [a Manhattan pediatrician], "those receptors send a signal to the brain that suppresses the production of melatonin and keeps kids from feeling tired. And adolescents are low on melatonin and start producing it later to begin with."

The problems resulting from student sleep deprivation include:

- Behavior mimicking the symptoms of ADHD (being unable to sit still and focus in class or when working on homework)
- Roller-coaster emotions and impulses
- Increased anger outbursts
- Increased risk for anxiety and depression

The repercussions are so extensive that doctors may attempt to treat problems caused by sleep deprivation—such as by prescribing Adderall or Vyvanse for ADHD, for example—which can intensify the lack of sleep when ADHD may not be the primary problem after all. What teens need, in fact, is more routine high-quality sleep.

Taking smartphones away from teens isn't easy, however, since they were born into the iPhone era. Take my small grandchildren as an example. Starting from about one or one and a half years old, they've aggressively reached for someone's phone, determined to take possession, as if the device is the last drop of water on earth. And, if they get their hands on one, they know just what to do with it because they have observed since birth the attention everyone gives to these handhelds. When viewed from that lens, the concept of making a child wait until their eleventh birthday to get their smartphone shows a decade of parental patience. It's just that once the phone is in the child's hands, there's no turning back. They get safety and education at their fingertips, accidental viewing of pornography, hours of distraction from the world around them, sleep interference, potential contact with drug pushers, and mental health anguish from apps that can distort their view of reality and themselves.

The risks seemingly far outweigh the advantages. Yet here we are, with every middle school across America filled with a generation of smartphone addicts who deserve lives of joy and wellbeing. But we are nonetheless seeing their odds of joy reduced with each misplaced moment of screen time. That's because devices and apps have many imprisoned. And while the issues and repercussions are complex, the solution is not. But we can't merely give in; rather, students need help to navigate device usage in healthy ways. So don't give in and think there's nothing you can do. We humans were built to regenerate with rest, and it's more important in our years of development than at any other time in our life span. If there's one gift you can give your child, it's helping them get more sleep. One day, they'll thank you for having made the effort.

Here are some tips for helping your teen sleep:

- Don't preach and pressure your child to sleep; engage them in the conversation about its importance and share research about sleep's benefits.
- Let your child become part of the solution. Identify obstacles, including smartphone use and proximity at bedtime or caffeine consumption.
- Help your child understand that the bed is not for homework or social time but for sleeping. Engage them in identifying desirable locations for other activities.

Parents can use educators' help in fighting back against teens' lack of sleep and life interruption due to extensive smartphone and social media use. Remember, it's about how we communicate with students. They don't like authority figures telling them what to do, but they are smart, and they listen when presented insights and solutions that appeal to them. In the classroom, many teaching moments can be provided across all subjects to engage students in talking about how they learn, how and when they thrive, and the distractions they face. Educators can use research to stoke the conversation, sharing how students' sleep behavior is affected and how that distracts from learning and their lives beyond the classroom.

If we can involve students in the learning and discussion at an early age, like when they get smartphones, the odds increase that they can better learn to manage the potential negative effects. It's hardly radical thinking, either, since we wouldn't dare let a teen drive a car without proper training; it's too dangerous. Smartphones and social media pose dangers as well, and students need education and engagement from the moment they get a device to help them understand how to best manage its impact on their lives.

TAKEAWAYS

- Social media apps are primary forms of illegal drug pushing and buying.
- Eating disorders have a direct relationship with social media for many who suffer.
- Parents purchase smartphones for their children at age eleven, on average, for safety and education. They should consider also providing ongoing discussion and engagement around the device's risks, particularly sleep deprivation, and involve their children in finding ways to use the phone in healthy ways.

4

NOT YOUR FATHER'S (OR MOTHER'S) MARIJUANA

We've been duped about marijuana, parents and children alike.

It's not about legality. Legal, not legal—that's for someone else to debate. It's also not about whether marijuana has value or not. We know marijuana (cannabis) has substantiated medical benefits and that many people use it recreationally and walk away with no harm. But problems often arise with street marijuana, leading to dire consequences for many students (and adults).

Marijuana has been a potent part of our culture for decades, and that's not about to change. But in the march to legality, messaging absorbed by students and parents is that marijuana is not problematic.

The facts reveal a different story, however. And every parent needs this information now.

Let me explain.

When I grew up in the 1980s in the college town of Oxford, Mississippi, with a population of less than ten thousand,
a consistent subject of our jokes and fascination involved our
community marijuana field. Shrouded behind a twelve-foot-tall
chain-link fence topped with barbed wire and a green curtain
that ran the length of the fence, keeping everything on the inside out of sight, the marijuana field belonged to the University
of Mississippi's National Center for Natural Products Research
(NCNPR).

It was one of the only legal marijuana fields in the country at the time, and researchers there emerged as some of the
foremost experts in the nation because they cultivated and then
tested marijuana in almost every reasonable manner to learn
about its potency and usefulness. As experts with the latest
equipment for testing the potency of THC, the ingredient in
marijuana that makes one high, the NCNPR scientists invited
law enforcement agencies from throughout the United States to
send in samples of marijuana confiscated from drug busts to be
studied. By receiving and testing these street marijuana samples over many years, the NCNPR collected valuable data that
shows a steady increase of potency in the marijuana circulating
in this country. In 1995, for example, the NCNPR reported
that the THC potency of street marijuana in America averaged
nearly 4 percent. By 2021, though, the average potency of street
marijuana tested across the country was nearly 16 percent. This
means the strength of street marijuana in America has increased
almost 400 percent over twenty-six years.

A nearly 400 percent increase. That's not a typo. That
number also doesn't reflect the fact that many chronic marijuana users today are much more sophisticated in maximizing
the impact of that 400 percent stronger THC. Sophisticated

extraction, distillation, and purification methods mean that many marijuana products on the street are 70 to 90 percent THC. Oils used in vape pens, for instance, often contain 70 to 90 percent THC, and the vaping itself delivers more potent highs and side effects, according to a 2018 John Hopkins Medicine study.

"Results showed that a few minutes after smoking, those who vaped the 25-milligram THC dosage reported an average of 77.5 on the overall strength of the drug's effect, meaning how high they felt compared with the average score of 66.4 reported by those who smoked the same dose," the report found. "Participants who vaped 25 milligrams of THC reported about a 7 percent higher score on average for anxiety and paranoia, compared with people who smoked the same amount of the compound. Those who vaped any dose of THC also reported higher levels of dry mouth and dry eyes than those who smoked it. For example, when vaping 25 milligrams of THC, the participants rated dry mouth at 67.1 on average compared with 42.6 for those smoking it."

Consider, then, that the oils students are vaping are 70 to 90 percent THC, often extracted from marijuana nearly 400 percent stronger than 1995 marijuana, and the problem becomes apparent.

"It's like comparing the original Coca-Cola, which had a small amount of coca leaf extract, to crack cocaine—it's a new ball game," is how a scientist with the NCNPR explained it to me.

It's no coincidence that a 2022 study published in the *Lancet*, among the world's oldest peer-reviewed medical journals, concluded that higher concentrations of THC in marijuana worldwide make marijuana more addictive and that people who use it are more likely to suffer mental health issues, including depression, anxiety, and psychosis. The authors concluded that "use of high potency cannabis, compared to low potency cannabis, was linked to a four-fold increased risk of addiction." The study also found that as marijuana potency has increased, cases of marijuana-associated psychosis, "loss of contact with reality," have already increased.

No, this is not your father's (or mother's) marijuana. A scientist with the NCNPR told me that, while the center doesn't have official data dating back to 1965, it's believed that street marijuana then was likely 2 percent THC, half of the 1995 potency. That means most parents today have no idea what their children face using street marijuana. No concept. And many students themselves are duped, unsure of what's happening to them or why. I hear it all the time, and it's the single most surprising thing I've learned from the many students I get to engage with from throughout the country.

MARIJUANA AND TEENS

(Source: SAMHSA)

The Substance Abuse and Mental Health Services Administration (SAMHSA) provides the following facts about marijuana:

> Marijuana refers to the dried leaves, flowers, stems, and seeds from the *Cannabis sativa* or *Cannabis*

indica plant. It is a psychoactive drug that contains close to 500 chemicals, including THC, a mind-altering compound that causes harmful health effects. Marijuana use is prevalent among teens and young adults, and according to SAMHSA's 2018 National Survey on Drug Use and Health, an estimated 3.1 million youths ages 12–17 reported using marijuana in 2018.

Marijuana use among teens tends to increase with age. While 1.8 percent of youths ages 12–13 reported consuming marijuana in the past year, that number increased to 11.3 percent of those ages 14–15 and 23.4 percent by ages 15–16.

Marijuana can be consumed in a variety of ways—including smoking, vaping, oils, teas, and edibles. Edibles have become popular because people can mix marijuana into their favorite foods, such as brownies, cookies, and candy. However, edibles are dangerous because they can lead to accidental ingestion or overconsumption. Since it takes longer to digest edibles and feel their effects, people may consume more at one time to expedite that process.

There is also "synthetic marijuana," a man-made drug that goes by names including Spice, K2, or Herbal Incense. K2/Spice is a mixture of plant materials sprayed with synthetic psychoactive chemicals and is labeled "not for human consumption."

"Ah, Mr. Magee," a student will say after hearing me talk about how marijuana today is 400 percent stronger, posing addiction and mental health risks. "I've always heard marijuana is not addictive, but I'm addicted. I thought maybe something was wrong with me. I'm using too much, morning, noon, and night, and it's slowing down my life and affecting my health. And I think, *I'll quit. Tomorrow, I'll quit.* But I keep using it."

"Don't get fooled by the fact that states are legalizing marijuana," I'll explain. "Alcohol is legal, but what if you drank a fifth of vodka daily? How functional and healthy would you be?"

The student will give a half smile, or more of a smirk.

"Not at all."

"That's right. With marijuana, you are effectively drinking a fifth a day."

With daily marijuana consumption, most users don't get the same feelings they once did with the drug. It's like alcohol, opiates, or anything else—after sustained use, the user develops a tolerance.

"I don't even feel much from it anymore," a student told me, echoing the sentiment of so many others. "I get a little tingly, or maybe it messes with my mind, and I want to take it easy. But that's it. It's just, I can't quit."

After I delivered this message to seven hundred college fraternity members, rising sophomores and juniors, from throughout the country during a summer leadership conference, a young man wearing a T-shirt, flip-flops, and a stylish cap pulled down over bushy hair approached.

"Can you guess where I'm from?" he said, extending his hand for a warm greeting.

"California?"

"You got it, brother," he said.

"Cal," he said. "Cal Berkeley."

I smiled, bracing for what I assumed would be a verbal laceration for sharing less-than-flattering information about marijuana.

"I'm not anti-pot," I said.

"I know. I didn't get that at all. Your message is the best I've heard addressed to young people regarding marijuana."

I stood up taller, smiling broadly. "Keep talking."

"Those for legal marijuana will like what you have to say. You make a valid point. Street marijuana isn't what it used to be. I have so many friends who can't keep a job, aren't happy, sit around stoned and gaming most of the day and night, and don't know why.

"I'm for legal marijuana because what you say is right. It's unregulated, and it's addictive. There's research to back this up, and it's undeniable, but that message gets lost in the legalization argument. We're so busy saying it's not harmful, but alcohol is legal and incredibly harmful."

"If this wasn't post-COVID, I'd give you a hug," I said.

He smiled, opened his arms wide and leaned in, before wrapping them tightly around my shoulders. "Keep talking," he said. "My generation needs to hear this."

Parents often ask me if there's anything I learn from students that surprises me, and I respond that I'm always stunned when, after I talk about more potent street marijuana and its risks, students, usually male, approach and explain how marijuana is stealing their joy. They say that they hear it is nonaddictive but they try to quit and can't, and they describe how it controls their life. They say they don't know how to do anything without some THC in their system. Similarly, I'm always surprised that parents tell me that when they learned their middle or high school teens were regularly using marijuana, they didn't like it, but they also weren't that upset. They assumed it was what teens do and there was little they could do about it. And then I remember, that's exactly how I was with my sons, William and Hudson, in high school. I didn't like it, but I didn't understand how things had changed either.

WHAT STUDENT CANNABIS USE DISORDER (CUD) LOOKS LIKE

It went something like this: When William, our oldest, was in the ninth grade, my wife, Kent, found crudely made paraphernalia—a sports drink bottle with a straw sealed into the top with tape—in his closet the night after he'd had a friend sleep over. I sat William down after dinner for a talk (unaware of the pitiful example I was setting as I held a glass of red wine in my hand) and asked him why he was willing to risk his promising high school career in academics and sports by using illegal drugs.

William glared back at me, and I wondered what he was thinking. I kept up the questions until he finally gave a response. "It's just weed," he said. "It's about to be legal everywhere. Studies say it's good for you."

"It's illegal," I said. "Besides, cigarettes are legal. That doesn't mean you should smoke. Tar and nicotine are harmful to you."

"I don't want to smoke, Dad. Besides, I was just experimenting. I'm not gonna start doing it all the time."

I grounded William for two weeks for breaking the law and buying an illegal substance with money we had given him.

"I've seen friends in college think they could use illegal drugs and walk away, but they couldn't. Just be smart," I told him.

A year later, we noticed William was carrying a lighter in his pocket. We heard from other parents that he and his peers were using marijuana. But he was getting good grades, excelling in track and field, and actively participating in a church youth group. His friends were the type you'd want your child to have—intelligent, caring, active, and ambitious. What I didn't know, however, is that they used marijuana occasionally. I'd learn later that William, and a couple of his friends, began using it daily. What I didn't know is that by the time William arrived at college he used marijuana several times a day, every day. What I didn't know is that he lettered on the track team of a Southeastern Conference university and made A's in the honors college *at the same time* that he was under the influence of powerful marijuana. And while his college record looked impressive, the substance was taking a toll on his performance and mental clarity. What I didn't understand is that the low, persistent cough he attributed to allergies was instead caused by habitual marijuana use. "As with tobacco smoke, marijuana smoke has a toxic mixture of gases and tiny particles that can harm the lungs," says the National Institute on Drug Abuse. "Someone who smokes marijuana regularly may have many of the same breathing and lung problems as tobacco smokers, such as a daily cough."

I didn't know that because this marijuana was so much stronger than it was in my youth, it was taking control of his life. And what I also didn't think about was that if William was using so much illegal street marijuana regularly, he must have been getting it from drug dealers—dealers who sold other drugs.

That's how it went down, however, as we learned by reading the journal William kept in treatment after college, which was found in his apartment after he accidentally overdosed and died. The coroner's ruling was that William had alcohol, marijuana, benzos, and opiates in his system. The unofficial ruling is that he suffered from substance use disorder and he used an array of substances over the years, beginning in middle school. Still, the one constant was by far marijuana. By his late college years, smoking was such a part of his life that he didn't do much of anything without getting marijuana freshly into his system.

William told me during a breakfast we had together after treatment, when he was sober, that I was right about the warning I delivered that night when he was in the ninth grade.

"What do you mean?" I asked.

"I mean you warned me that even though they say marijuana is not addictive, you had friends who used it habitually in college and couldn't stop," he replied. "That was me, and I couldn't stop."

"Well," I said, "I wasn't exactly right. When it was apparent you were using drugs in high school, I didn't understand that you didn't need punishment and a lecture. You needed counseling or treatment. I'm sorry."

"I love you, Dad," he said.

I never saw William again after that day. Still, I frequently use the lessons learned from his experience with marijuana and other drugs and what we did and did not do as parents, just as I use the experience of our son Hudson, William's younger brother. Hudson, now more than a decade sober after nearly dying of an accidental drug overdose at a fraternity house on a university campus, allows me to share his story, and he sometimes shares it himself to help others. It's the journey of giving back that so many of us who have battled substance use disorder embark upon, because helping others also helps us make amends for it all.

Like William, Hudson began periodically using marijuana with friends in late middle school and early high school. He was convinced that because legalization seemed imminent in some areas and marijuana exhibited proven medicinal benefits for some afflictions, like treating nausea in cancer patients undergoing chemotherapy, the substance wasn't harmful, even to developing teenagers. He kept his use hidden; a second child is always more sophisticated at concealment. We'd suspected his use based on something we heard from his friends' parents, and when we asked, he'd deny it. Like most children, Hudson wanted to please us. Besides, he was the sweetest person, just like many are despite what substance use disorder makes of them.

He seemed honest to us, and we believed him. Most parents believe their children because it's their innate desire to do so. We created them, and we want to shape them into images we view as better than our own images. Illegal substance use will make liars of most of them, however. Still, parents will say, "I'm so thankful our child is honest with us." But I think even the most honest children are rarely candid with their parents, because it's difficult being honest with themselves. They don't want to do so-called wrongs. It's just that they don't always know how not to do them. So they'll deny the behavior in order to remain in their parents' good graces and continue to enjoy privileges like a phone, a car, money, and going out with friends, and they'll deny doing wrong while looking straight into their parents' eyes.

What's a parent to do?

We didn't catch on that our son Hudson had fallen into daily marijuana use in high school until his senior year, even though it had occurred regularly since early high school. He was a good soccer player and participated in year-round soccer on one of the best travel teams in the South from middle school into high school. Knowing he had so much invested in the sport, we were stunned during his senior year when he skipped out on a regular-season midweek game to ride around with friends and smoke some supposedly highly potent marijuana a friend had obtained. Unaware of the skip plan, I'd traveled to the out-of-town game, an hour away, only to be shocked when Hudson wasn't on the sideline. I knew he'd left for school that morning. But all along, Hudson and his friends had had a plan. Later that night, I confronted my son, who admitted he'd skipped both school and the soccer game to hang out with friends for a senior skip day.

"Did y'all drink?"

"A little," he said.

"Did y'all smoke marijuana?"

"No," he said.

We handed him a home drug test, and he took it, giving us the result.

Positive.

"Why didn't you just tell us?"

"I didn't want to let you down."

If this story is troubling, don't feel sorry for us as parents or for Hudson, our son, who has become one of the most important role models in my life. More than a decade sober, he helps me understand what teens go through—navigating parents, activities, and marijuana, among other distractions. He's one of the most honorable humans I know, and sharing his story is difficult only because I don't want others to get the wrong idea about him. But parents need to know—they are not alone.

Substances do bad things to good people, and your child will stand before you, look you in the eyes, and lie because they are ashamed and love you and are in over their head with a potent substance. Hudson checked into intensive outpatient program for substance use disorder once he was released from the hospital after nearly dying from an overdose at his fraternity house. He'd been in a coma for two days, and the doctor told us he was likely brain dead. I was counting the days, imagining how long we would wait before pulling the plug, when he woke up. Once he regained consciousness, it was clear he didn't have brain damage. He was just confused because the substances he'd been misusing still clouded his mind. Hudson had nearly died, yet he still didn't think he needed treatment.

"I'm not addicted to anything," he said initially. "I just made a mistake, and I won't do it again."

Days later, he agreed he needed treatment. Weeks later, his mind had cleared, and he explained how he'd become addicted to marijuana and alcohol and had added Xanax and other substances in college. Our family was going through a difficult time—there were marriage and career struggles due to my substance use disorder—and my wife and I had tightened up on the money we gave Hudson for college. He'd made his own spending money by selling marijuana to fraternity brothers and friends at other fraternities.

"I'd walk to class and pass all these guys high-fiving me and calling out my name," Hudson recalled recently. "I thought I was popular, like I had all these friends. It wasn't until years later, with a clear mind, that I could look back and see reality.

They weren't my friends, and they all knew me because I was getting them weed."

The first weeks, months, and years of Hudson's sobriety provided head-turning revelations that kept us delighted; it was like watching a man mature emotionally at high speed. Do you know how they say habitual marijuana use starting at a young age stunts emotional growth? Yes, indeed, it does. Both our sons suffered that consequence, but with Hudson, we got to watch the rapid healing in real time, and there are few things I've enjoyed watching in life more than that. It gave us a window into the damage that daily use of strong marijuana does to a developing teen. Hudson became good at things he didn't know he was good at, and he enjoyed people and things he didn't think he would. He became instantly one of the most honest people I know and became genuinely kind and engaged with others. And through that honesty—absolute honesty—we learned so much that we hadn't known. For example, when Hudson and his friends in high school made a marijuana purchase together, he noticed that he was different because when they all checked their supply the following weekend, his was all gone. "I knew I was different but didn't understand what that meant," he said.

It's frightening to look back and see how much marijuana use stole from Hudson, our son William, and therefore our family. After treatment, William told us that he'd come to almost every family holiday dinner high on marijuana, and it was what most of his friends did, too.

"Is that a thing?" I asked.

"Yep."

William explained that he'd had the marijuana bug worse than most of his friends, so while they may have shown up at the dinner table high, he'd shown up trashed. And we hadn't even known, beyond the fact that I remember awkward conversations with him on what should have been the happiest family days.

It's also scary to realize that those experiences with our sons occurred more than a decade ago. Marijuana is even more potent today, and vaping wasn't a thing then. But marijuana use and the vaping of marijuana are on the rise, according to a recent study from Columbia University that reveals increased use, particularly among students who "socialize a lot without supervision" as opposed to those who participate in "structured activities."

Almost every student in high school or college I talk to who's struggling with substance misuse faces a marijuana problem deeply embedded within their disorder. Most of the students understand the situation, but almost none of their parents get it. Most parents don't like their children's marijuana use, but they are stuck in the perception from their younger days that most street marijuana is mild and therefore not too harmful, and they reason that it's getting legalized, so how bad can it be?

Well, trust me. It can be very destructive.

Consider the university student I connected with who helped me fundraise to create the William Magee Center at Ole Miss. Richard was ambitious, destined for law school, and respected by fellow fraternity members who elected him one of three officers in charge of their annual philanthropy. He helped me bring in more than $25,000 for that year and years to come. We became friends, occasionally getting lunch, and he shared with me about his father's alcohol and drug abuse, explaining how it had taken his family's joy.

"I don't hate my father for it," he said. "I know he's sick. But I don't ever want to do that to my family."

Late in his senior year, with law school on the horizon, Richard asked me to meet for lunch. We did, though he didn't have much of an appetite. "I'm struggling," he said. "I started using marijuana in high school. My usage became habitual in college. I don't drink much, and I don't normally do other drugs. But this stuff is making me crazy. I try to back off, and I have withdrawal symptoms a day or two later . . . I'm depressed. I go back and do more, and I'm depressed because I've failed. It is ruining my life."

I explained to Richard that his life was not ruined. All that was lost was the past. Today and tomorrow were right there to seize, to take responsibility for, to enjoy. "Today is not ruined," I said. "Not at all."

I told him he needed substance treatment help.

"I'm not an addict," he said.

"You are not?"

"I'm struggling with marijuana. They'd laugh me out of there if I showed up saying I was addicted to marijuana."

It was the first time I'd seen into the young mind to find young fear. This student and his peers had positioned marijuana as a mild drug, and thus viewed succumbing to marijuana as weak—something you didn't do.

I'd love to tell you that I talked Richard into treatment. Frankly, I never brought down the wall he put up between marijuana and addiction. I tried to get him into counseling, hoping that might reduce that barrier, but no luck. Last I heard, Richard had nearly finished law school and was still struggling—advancing along a predictable path while truly enjoying very little of the journey. I'm hopeful, however, that one day he'll get there. One day, with a bit more maturity, he will understand that almost any substance can bring us down. There's no shame in admitting that street marijuana is often an addictive drug, powerful enough to transform the most promising young person into a joyless robot who is continually looking toward the next hit.

"I didn't have the drive to do much," one student told me about his condition after years of daily marijuana use that left him in a perpetual fog. "I felt lazy, like I was a procrastinator and not worth much. I felt sluggish, and watching movies or gaming was easier."

The National Institute on Drug Abuse (NIDA) says that marijuana is addictive and that the odds for addiction increase substantially for those who begin use in their teens. Furthermore, those who use marijuana daily face odds of developing addiction of up to 50 percent. Even for teens who don't become addicted, NIDA notes that marijuana use is problematic for learning and mental health—and that for many who use it hoping to reduce anxiety, it actually increases anxiety, among other negative side effects.

"Marijuana is linked to school failure," NIDA states. "Marijuana's negative effects on attention, memory, and learning can last for days and sometimes weeks—especially if you use it often. Someone who smokes marijuana daily may have a 'dimmed-down' brain most or all of the time."

A dimmed-down brain is not something most teens want; it's not among the reasons they give for using illegal drugs.

WHY STUDENTS USE MARIJUANA

These are some of the reasons (in no particular order) that students say they use marijuana. They use it to:

1. Change how they feel (to escape and to self-medicate for anxiety or depression)
2. Mimic others (parents; peers; those in media, including music and movies)
3. Fit in with friends
4. Fight boredom
5. Rebel against authority
6. Find instant gratification
7. Deal with a lack of confidence

In addition to having these reasons for using, they are also misinformed about marijuana's effects.

Charlie, a fifth-year senior in college finishing his last two classes, asked me to meet for coffee. "I have so much to say to you," he said. I hadn't seen Charlie in twelve weeks, since he'd sat alongside his father and peered at me with hazy eyes as I explained he needed to check into substance treatment. Charlie had disagreed and had insistently explained to his father how he would "stop." Charlie was similar to my William, in that he is tenderhearted, had graduated from a prestigious private high school, and had attended church youth group regularly and a summer Christian camp until the tenth grade, but ended up with a marijuana addiction and ultimately became hooked on fentanyl.

"I was so mad at you," Charlie told me at the coffee shop, sitting in the same chair from which he had peered angrily at me twelve weeks earlier. "I kept trying to make my father believe that I could handle this, that I could get it under control. Every time before, I'd talked him into that. But not this time."

"You almost did," I reminded Charlie. "I had talked your father into taking you to treatment, but when I got home a couple of hours later, he texted me and said you'd talked him into staying at your college. I texted him back and said, 'That's fine, just be prepared to never see your son again.'"

"I know," Charlie said. "That got him. And he got me to treatment. That's why I'm here. I want to thank you—I'm twelve weeks sober and I've never been happier. I know it's just the beginning, but it's a beginning and it feels so good."

I asked Charlie to explain his descent from having everything to having a fentanyl addiction.

"I started in middle school with prescription Adderall," he said. "I didn't like it, but my mother made me take it because it helped me make all A's. I don't blame her for it. She just wanted the best for me. I have attention deficit disorder, so it was either B's with some C's without Adderall or all A's with it.

"But they had me on a high dosage. I didn't like taking it because it dulled my personality. So some days I'd skip it, but other days I'd double up. Eventually they moved me to Vyvanse, saying it was lower risk for addictive behavior, but it wasn't much different.

"The problem is that once I had my pill for the day, I couldn't look away from schoolwork, but I hated how it felt coming down off it and I couldn't get to sleep, so I started using a lot of marijuana to counteract it. When I was off Adderall or Vyvanse, I liked marijuana okay and used it some. But when I was on the prescription, I couldn't get enough marijuana—it's like I was a marijuana-inhaling monster because I needed enough to counteract the high stimulant prescription.

"I couldn't see myself as a habitual marijuana user, but that's what I had become. Things got bad when the drug dealer selling me marijuana offered me a Percocet. I thought, *Why not? Just one time*. But it wasn't one time. Then those Percocet pills became counterfeit pills, or fentanyl. I quickly got in over my head."

Charlie explained that he went through supervised withdrawal at the treatment center but that he did it without the use of medications like Suboxone. "I was shaking so bad," he said. "It was violent, awful. But I'm glad I did it that way because when I think about using, I remember that."

"So, what about the ADD? Are your still treating that?"

"I couldn't go back on Vyvanse. It's not for me. My doctor told me about Strattera, a nonstimulant ADD medication. I tried that and it's been good. Different, but good. Here's how I explain it to friends, relating it to my love of fishing.

"On 80 milligrams of Vyvanse like I was taking, I'd go on a six-hour fishing trip with friends and keep pushing for eight hours, trying to catch one more again and again. I couldn't stop. Without taking Adderall or Vyvanse, I'd go fishing for six hours and my ADD would kick in and I'd end up fishing for two hours, swimming part of the time, and stopping to read my phone. On Strattera, I'll go fishing on a six-hour trip and end up fishing for four hours, which seems about perfect. It helps me stay focused, but not unnaturally."

"Do you still crave marijuana?"

"No," Charlie said.

TIPS FOR NAVIGATING MARIJUANA

- Ask your child what they know about marijuana. Listen carefully and attentively, without strong reactions.

- Explain to your child the health risks of marijuana, including its impact on the brain (which doesn't fully develop until a person is in their twenties).
- Tell your child about the potency of street marijuana and the increased risk of addiction.
- Drug test if in doubt.
- Seek counseling sooner rather than later if warnings signs appear.

LEGAL OR ILLEGAL— DOES IT EVEN MATTER?

You are mistaken if you have concluded by this point that I'm against legal or medical marijuana. Marijuana is not for me, because mind-altering substances don't benefit me and therefore have no helpful place in my life. I'm not anti-marijuana, however. As stated previously in this chapter, it's clear marijuana has some medicinal benefits. So do most drugs, if used responsibly and appropriately. I have a friend who struggled with alcohol and cocaine to the point that it ended his career and relationships. He went to treatment and stopped using those drugs but settled in with marijuana as a sort of next-best option, and, for him, it's worked. For twenty years, he's done well professionally and avoided alcohol and cocaine. It likely helps that he's a musician, so he doesn't need a lot of drive to get to the office and push through eight hours of work. Still, for him, marijuana has provided a life for two decades when alcohol and cocaine were taking everything away. I have other friends who occasionally use marijuana recreationally, and have done so off and on since college, much like the casual alcohol drinker. And I know individuals who have received medical benefits from marijuana, like relief from nausea during chemotherapy. So I'm not here to make a case against medical marijuana's role or even recreational marijuana's role in our country. Alcohol is legal, but it, too, is damaging when misused.

I make this point emphatically because the movement to legalize marijuana involves some passionate, if not passionately aggressive, types who attack anyone who says anything negative about marijuana. Perhaps that's why middle school, high school, and college students don't know the truth about marijuana—because many are scared to speak up.

There's no avoiding the truth, however, and the fact is that marijuana is addictive and potentially quite damaging to developing teens and college students. Let's not bury that lede any longer, for the children's sake.

What, then, are parents to do when 22 percent of high school seniors and 8 percent of eighth graders have vaped marijuana in the past year (according to a 2020 survey from NIDA)? It's not easy, let's say that. Strong-willed students are hard to manage at times. But we know some tactics work better than others.

For instance, it doesn't work to just say, "No, you can't do marijuana or you are in trouble." Remember, they've already learned plenty about marijuana from peers and the media. They need education and reasoning, and it's best to begin providing this early in middle school if not before. Don't turn your nose up at marijuana or those who use it. Instead, ask your child what's important to them and whether it includes doing well in school, having a sharp mind, and experiencing joy. Most students will affirm that academic performance, clear-mindedness, and joy are things they want. Ask them what they know about marijuana, then talk to them about facts—marijuana's impact on the developing mind, its addictive potential, and its other side effects. Ask them if they are okay with marijuana taking away what they love, their joy.

I'm reminded of a father and his son, a junior in college, whom I met with at the beginning of a fall semester. The student was making decent grades as an accounting major, was in a "good" fraternity, and had a girlfriend acing premed. Oh, and he also kept up two part-time jobs, helping pay his way. The one big problem: years of daily, habitual marijuana use that had stolen his joy.

The substance misuse had not yet cost the student his girlfriend, though she was growing weary of his stoned and yawny demeanor. Nor had it cost him the drive to study or work part-time jobs. But almost everything else he had previously enjoyed in life—like playing tennis and basketball with friends, hiking, and quality family time—marijuana had stolen. In other words, he still looked good on paper, but he didn't care much about anything on that paper.

The student's father, also, had had enough.

"This isn't an intervention," the father turned to his son and said, as I sipped my coffee and nearly choked. I'd come for a meet and greet, unprepared for intervening with a student I didn't yet know. "But I've had enough. I don't want you using illegal drugs any longer. It's taking my son away from me."

I smiled at the student. He yawned, covering his mouth.

"Long night last night?" I asked.

He stares back in response.

"Listen," I said. "Your father is right. If he's had enough, he's wise to express that. Here's the deal, though: How do you feel? Do you like that the marijuana holds you hostage daily? Is that something you want to continue?

"Trust me, I meet students every now and then who say, 'Yes, absolutely, this is the life I want.' So that's what I'm asking you: What do you want? If you want a life structured around marijuana use and its toll on your brain, you can seize that life more vigorously than you are doing now. It's just a matter of what you want. It's not what your father wants or what I want."

Then I asked, "Do you like accounting?"

"Well, I suggested it for him," the father said, interrupting.

"Of course, you did," I said. "When I found my William dead from an accidental overdose, I found the journal he kept while in treatment. In that journal he wrote the words 'my dad made most of my decisions for me.'"

Ouch.

Except William was right. I did. It was done with the best intentions. I wanted him to have everything, to use his talents to shine in the world. I should have spent more time letting my growing son know that I cared only about his joy and that I wanted to help him find and keep that.

"Do you like accounting?" I repeated my question.

"That's a good question," the student said.

"Do you love your girlfriend?" I said.

"Yes," he said, sitting up.

"Okay, then, how does she feel about your marijuana use?"

"She doesn't like it."

"Now we are getting somewhere. You want to keep your girlfriend, but you aren't sure about accounting. What about joy? Do you want joy?"

"Yes," he said.

"Do you think marijuana steals your joy?"

He nodded yes.

"So you want to choose both joy and your girlfriend, and marijuana use threatens both of those, but you aren't sure yet that you want to stop? Or is it that you've used marijuana for so long that you don't know how to stop?"

He nodded yes, dropping his head.

"Listen, son, I know you feel ashamed to answer that, but you shouldn't feel ashamed. I suffer from substance use disorder and so do many of the people I respect most in this world. If you want joy, I'll point you in the right direction, toward treatment that can help you start on that journey."

He nodded yes.

The father, sitting next to him, smiled broadly. "I've been fighting this for years. How did you get there so quickly?"

"It's not that I'm a miracle worker," I explained. "Your son has a long journey ahead. Let's see if he dives in and does the hard work. But how I got you there within fifteen minutes of first meeting him was by not telling him he's failing and letting me down. I just asked a simple question: What do you want?"

It's easier for students to envision how substances are taking away what they want. But when they feel shame, they are more inclined to promise to stop, then watch you drive away and reach for the baggie of marijuana. We've got to meet them on their terms and have conversations that they engage with to help them get on the road to wellbeing.

And we need to get the messages to students sooner rather than later. If this young man had seen marijuana as a substance that could take from him rather than give, would he have gone down this path? It's hard to know for sure, but certainly the odds are increased that he would not have.

When teens habitually use marijuana, it's a red flag for more trouble ahead. Consider immediate counseling. Also, you have a right to periodically drug test your child, and if they continue use, consider substance treatment. Consequences are essential, but will not work well alone. Counseling works and can make a difference, so don't be afraid to use it when needed.

Most importantly, remember that your children need you to help them navigate. You got them to swimming lessons, and you weren't afraid to give tips on driving. They'll hear a lot of incorrect information about marijuana, but if you get involved early on, sharing information and not judgment, the odds will improve for the best outcome.

If your children have begun using marijuana already, the aim is to reduce or eliminate use. The more days they spend with a clear mind while their brains and emotions continue developing, the greater chance they'll have for a lifetime of joy ahead.

TAKEAWAYS

- Today's street marijuana is 300 to 400 percent stronger than it was twenty-five years ago, and it's nearly four times as addictive. It can cause mental health issues including anxiety, depression, and psychosis.
- People who begin using marijuana early in life have a 50 percent greater chance of becoming addicted.
- Children are inherently good, but when it comes to marijuana use, they may feel shame and guilt and lie about whether they are using despite the evidence.
- Marijuana is illegal for teens in every state, except

medical marijuana in some states. Those using the drug are obtaining it from dealers who will likely peddle other, more potent substances.

- Less is more—as in no use or less use—when it comes to allowing students' brains and behaviors to develop.

5

ALCOHOL NATION

When it comes to teaching our children about alcohol and its risks, we're better at it than we are with marijuana only because we tend to have more experience with the substance. We discount that knowledge, however, when we excessively romanticize alcohol and obsess over it, which counteracts our efforts to educate our children.

We've taught students, for instance, to avoid the most lethal alcohol-related danger—drinking and driving. Teaching them not to get behind the wheel and drive is a big win, considering that decades ago young people in this country thought nothing of driving while intoxicated. I remember my first big high school party. I was in the ninth grade and a friend drove us there. Inside a clubhouse, a band was playing. Partygoers danced, waving around plastic cups of various drinks they'd mixed in the parking lot. Once the band finished, many gathered in the parking lot, talking and drinking until the police drove up, ordering everyone to disperse. Drinkers started their cars and drove away.

This is not the case today. At a teenage party where there's lots of drinking, revelers will now hail Uber rides, get rides from sober friends, or have their parents pick them up. But most won't get in the car and drive themselves home. Although too many teens still drive drunk, the percentage has drastically declined over the years. Even though alcohol remains the top drug of choice for teens, strict laws and education have diminished such behavior.

We can thank Mothers Against Drunk Driving (MADD) for helping this country see the light: education and toughened laws for drunk driving have reduced arrests and senseless deaths, many of which were partly due to uneven legislation across states. For example, in Louisiana eighteen-year-olds could purchase alcohol, while in neighboring Mississippi eighteen-year-olds could purchase only beer, not hard liquor; meanwhile, in some other states, twenty-one was the age limit for purchasing any type of alcohol. Such inequities were common, and MADD noted that drunk drivers crossed state lines, wrecked their cars, and killed themselves or others. Concerned mothers formed MADD in 1980, when teen drinking and drunk driving deaths were at an all-time high. By 1984 the organization had widespread legislative support in Washington, and the National Minimum Drinking Age Act became law, raising the legal drinking age uniformly across America to the age of twenty-one. Insurance company leaders rejoiced because automobile accidents decreased by 16 percent and drunk driving deaths by 40 percent, as the legislation combined with much stricter state penalties (in most states, several DUI offenses became a felony).

Regardless of the strides that have been made, it's important to acknowledge that we do a poor job in America of positioning alcohol as a substance that can cause pain and damage beyond drinking and driving. Instead, we lift up alcohol as if it's a juice of the gods, magically bringing celebratory joy into our lives whenever consumed. Think about it: so much of what we do for fun revolves around alcohol. Super Bowl party? Booze it up. Anniversary celebration? Here's to you. Professional accomplishment? Cheers. Tailgating for a college (or high school) game? Pack the cooler. Also, the wiser we get in America, and the more money we make, the more alcohol we consume. Yes, that's a fact. Consider that more than 72 percent of college graduates in this country drink alcohol, and more than 81 percent of those earning more than $100,000 in annual income do, according to a 2021 Gallup survey, while in comparison 60 percent of all U.S. adults consume alcohol.

It's no surprise, then, that children today have their first drink on average at eleven for boys and thirteen for girls, even though the legal drinking age across the country is twenty-one. There's irony in the fact that in 1965 research showed that adolescents started to drink at an average age of seventeen and a half. That's about the age at which they went to college, where many students started drinking as a rite of passage. Yet, in the years since, the initial drinking age has dropped.

It's not, however, as if most children have their first drink at a young age and swiftly move to daily consumption. Because the drinking age is twenty-one, alcohol is a difficult substance for teens to consume regularly. A teen can more easily hide smoking marijuana or taking a pill. Still, the smell of alcohol is detectable along with the behavior it can create, so most teens are more apt to drink when clearly away from authority figures for a prolonged period of time. And when their generation drinks, it drinks a lot, as if alcohol were the last water on earth. The official term is *binge drinking*—having four or more drinks in two hours for girls or five or more for boys. More than 90 percent of all alcohol consumed by young people (ages twelve to twenty) is consumed as binge drinking, according to the National Survey on Drug Use and Health conducted by SAMHSA in 2018. And teenage girls binge drink more than boys, whereas boys are more likely to use marijuana and other substances.

THE PROBLEM WITH BINGE DRINKING

Our parents told us nothing good happens after midnight. I tell students: Nothing good happens on a binge—nothing. Losing control of yourself never goes well.

Never.

The CDC says binge drinking, an intense drinking practice common among high school and college students, is "the most common, costly, and deadly pattern of excessive alcohol use in the United States."

These teens aren't sipping alcohol for the taste or the warm, fuzzy glow it provides. They drink fast and heavily to get drunk, in the way they've seen friends share about it on social media—see my drink, see me drunk, see me pictured all blurry now. And the older the teens get, the more likely and often they will binge.

Such behavior doesn't qualify as being an "alcoholic," someone who suffers from alcohol use disorder, primarily abusing alcohol regularly and developing a high tolerance. Yes, young binge drinkers have a higher chance statistically of suffering from substance use disorder, but binge drinking as a behavior qualifies only as risky substance behavior. And risky it is. On any college campus, the damage caused by binge drinking is incalculable. It results in missed classes, which can result in shame, which can result in depression, which can result in more missed classes, which can result in academic failure, which can result in family distress, financial and otherwise. It results in sexual assaults, sex that wouldn't have otherwise happened, and a myriad of other distressing behaviors that wouldn't have occurred if sober. It results in unintended injury, alcohol poisoning, violence, and more. For high school students, binge drinking can have some of the same results—and even worse, it's a gateway drug for many, given that other risky substances have more appeal when one is under the influence of alcohol.

Let's face it: you, like me, are a child of the alcohol nation, so compared to drugs, there's less I can tell you about alcohol that you don't know. The government and educating nonprofits will spend considerable ink explaining to you how much alcohol is in a drink and the signs to look for that show consumption or intoxication. But you know what under the influence looks and smells like. My concern is helping you understand more of what you don't quite know or understand, because that will better prepare you as a parent or educator to help children navigate this complicated world. Here are some of the most common questions I get from parents regarding alcohol and some answers that may help.

1. Is the national drinking age of twenty-one making teens' relationship with alcohol worse?
2. Should we consider the European model and let our children drink at sixteen?
3. Are parents responsible?
4. Can a struggling child who quits using other substances still drink?
5. What can parents do to delay and reduce alcohol use?

The short answers to these questions are (1) perhaps, (2) not according to research, (3) yes and no, (4) no, and (5) plenty. But let's dig in deeper.

Is the national drinking age of twenty-one making it worse in other ways for teens?

The effectiveness of the set drinking age is complicated. Suppose you ask officials from MADD or the CDC. In that case, they'll quickly cite undeniable evidence that drunk driving deaths have declined along with alcohol-related crashes due to the national age limit of twenty-one. Overall, teen drinking rates are perhaps also slightly lower.

This is undeniable evidence of benefit. Yet while lives have been saved, lives have perhaps also been ruined, as teen bingeing has soared since the drinking age of twenty-one went into effect in 1984. Maybe there's a direct connection, and maybe not. There's no denying that the alcohol behavior of teens and college students has grown riskier. The psychology of it might suggest that telling youths they can't have something might make them come in hard and strong for it when they get it.

That's why more than a decade ago, more than one hundred college and university presidents in this country created the Amethyst Initiative, supporting lowering the drinking age to eighteen. The group said it was against intoxication but supported responsible "adult" behavior with alcohol because the minimum drinking age of twenty-one wasn't working. The initiative cited in a statement the soaring, dangerous binge drinking on college campuses, saying twenty-one was not working, and campuses now faced a "culture of dangerous, clandestine binge-drinking"—often conducted off campus.

The statement further claimed, "Alcohol education that

mandates abstinence as the only legal option has not resulted in significant constructive behavioral change among our students. Adults under 21 are deemed capable of voting, signing contracts, serving on juries, and enlisting in the military, but are told they are not mature enough to have a beer."

The problem is not just the drinking but also the widespread fraud by otherwise law-abiding young citizens.

For example, I live in a small university city, Oxford, Mississippi. The city of Oxford has about 25,000 residents, while the adjacent University of Mississippi has about 22,000 students, the majority of whom are under the age of twenty-one. Most underage students in my college community and in others throughout the country arrive on campus with fake IDs. Even if they don't drink much, they want to get into bars and access the social scene. The bar owners and employees don't care if the ID is fake. They're just required to check, so they give a glance and serve away. I've long been troubled by this scenario because I know many of the students, and most are among the finest, most law-abiding citizens. They aren't the type to deliberately commit fraud under most circumstances. But they have left home, are on their own, and are old enough to enlist in the armed forces to fight for their country, and they prefer to commit fraud with a fake ID so they can join fellow students for drinks at the bar rather than sit at home, away from the party. Many parents are okay with this activity, believing it's a normal part of college life in this era. In most circumstances, parents would become shocked, if not disgusted, with their students for doctoring government documents to present a lie about themselves. Not so with the fake ID, however.

It's a troubling scenario, to say the least, but it's complicated because politically powerful lobbying groups, including MADD and insurance companies, don't agree that a lower drinking age is suitable for America's youth. Thus, parents today must navigate according to the laws in place.

For now, drinking alcohol under twenty-one in this country is illegal, and there are no signs that will be changing soon.

Should we consider the European model and let children drink at sixteen?

"Why don't we just invite our teens to the dinner table for wine or a beer like they do in Europe?"

I hear parents suggest this frequently. They say, "Europeans let them drink at sixteen and it's not a big deal."

It's not that simple, however.

Europe consumes the most alcohol globally, and most European countries have eighteen as the minimum legal drinking age. Some countries, including Austria, Belgium, Germany, and Switzerland, have a minimum drinking age of sixteen, which is what gets the most discussion among U.S. parents. These parents think that if alcohol is made less elusive, youth might be less inclined to binge dangerously. Multiple studies show, however, that European countries with the lowest legal drinking age also face alcohol binge rates among teens that are just as high, if not higher, than those in the U.S. It's a bit of an urban legend that teens in Europe don't struggle with alcohol, because the data from the World Health Organization suggests that younger teens in Europe drink more alcohol than their American peers and that European teens generally binge more than American teens. Additionally, total alcohol consumption by adults is higher in much of Europe than in the United States.

That's why many in the U.S. aren't interested in the Amethyst

Initiative or any groups trying to lower the drinking age. They argue that we indeed have a teen alcohol problem but the higher minimum drinking age of twenty-one helps keep the problem in check.

It's worth saying, however, that I have had more than a few college students tell me they began day-drinking and drinking daily with roommates and friends just because "they could"; they were still below the legal drinking age of twenty-one, but they lived alone or with peers, without parental supervision.

Mary Ann, a college student, explained how she and her sorority sisters, who lived together in an apartment during their sophomore year, began routinely pouring themselves a glass of wine each afternoon. "It felt adult," she said. Soon that glass become two glasses, and for one of her roommates, several. "That's what they call a rite of passage, I guess," she said. "Two of us could handle it but one couldn't. You just never know."

I explained that if all three had begun that habit in high school, perhaps more than one would have gotten into more than they could manage.

"Good point," Mary Ann said. "It's hard to know what's right, except that I know that's a bad habit we need to quit."

It was at that moment that I realized the value of simple education and discussion. Mary Ann was a college student, with ample education available about healthy habits, yet it didn't occur to her that this behavior might be harmful. She saw only that it was what you could do once you were living on your own—you could drink wine during the day and nobody was stopping you. But once she was able to think through the ramifications, through simple dialogue, she recognized it was not in her and her friends' best interest.

Are parents responsible?

I'd like to get you off the hook, I would. But parents play a critical role in their children's relationship with substance use and alcohol. No, you are not wholly responsible—students, beginning at puberty and through college, have their own minds and desires and often even our best efforts can't get in their way. However, parents can and do have influence, starting with genetics and including social and environmental factors.

According to the National Institute on Alcohol Abuse and Alcoholism (NIAAA), the following factors contribute to teen alcohol use. Notice how more than a couple intersect with parents in terms of DNA alone:

- Genetics
- Personality
- Rate of maturation and development
- Level of risk
- Social factors
- Environmental factors

Many parents think they'll help their children learn to drink. "Invite friends to drink in our house so we'll know you're safe and not driving." But the notion that you'll let your children drink in high school while just ensuring they don't drive is not wise. It's a common practice: parents decide to give in but try to be smart. It's not smart, however, unless you want to increase the odds that your child will suffer from substance use disorder later in life. That's because one thing we know about teen substance use is that less is better. It's important for parents to attend to each of these contributing factors because those who start drinking alcohol and using other substances like marijuana are statistically more likely to suffer from substance use disorder later in life.

This issue is the most difficult I see parents face, since almost every high school has at least one group of parents who say, "Our children are gonna do it, so I'd rather they do it safely in my house!" Other groups say, "It's illegal and I'm not going to support it."

Most of the college students I connect with whose parents let them drink all they wanted on weekends during high school as long as it was done safely in their home struggle mightily on campus with alcohol and other substances. Does that mean their parents may have saved their lives in high school by making sure they were drinking in their home with friends rather than drinking and then driving home? Perhaps. And I'm not judging these parents' decisions. Parents do what parents feel they must do. It's just that the more teens are allowed to drink illegally, the more they will likely drink or misuse other substances throughout life.

Some parents look for contextual reasons to let their children drink earlier, like believing they are more mature than others their age. For instance, a Penn State University study in 2021 found that parents of teens who go through early puberty are more likely to let their teens drink alcohol at an earlier age, believing they are mature enough to handle it. But that belief is not backed by research.

"A surprising proportion of parents in our study allowed their early-developing children to drink alcohol at the age of 14—in fact, one in seven," said Rebecca Bucci, a doctoral candidate in criminology at Penn State, according to a press release about the study. "It is important to remember that early puberty does not mean the child is more advanced in cognitive or brain development. They are not older in years or more socially mature. So allowing them freedoms common for young adults is risky."

Here's the fact all parents must remember about alcohol: the longer teens delay alcohol use, the better odds they have for a lifetime without addiction. In a speech, this line is so important that I repeat it, slowly, for effect: *The longer teens delay alcohol use, the better odds they have for a lifetime without addiction.*

It's that simple.

"Research shows that people who start drinking before the age of 15 are at a higher risk for developing alcohol use disorder later in life," according to the National Institute on Alcohol Abuse and Alcoholism. "For example, adults ages 26 and older who began drinking before age 15 are 5.6 times more likely to report having alcohol use disorder in the past year as those who waited until age 21 or later to begin drinking."

In addition to these environmental factors parents establish for their children, we know that genetics also plays a role in early and problematic drinking by teens. That's a direct link to parents, of course, relating to high-risk areas including rate of maturation and development, and personality. Even though these hand-me-down traits are not something parents can control, it's important to be aware of what your children might inherit from you, so you can get ahead of any associated risks by providing them more information and education or earlier counseling. Some women with mothers who received a breast cancer diagnosis will have a BRCA gene test; if a harmful mutation is found, they'll take steps, such as undergoing early and continuous screenings or having their breasts removed to lessen their chances of getting the disease. In the substance use disorder realm, if a thirteen-year-old reached puberty at age eleven, has ADHD, has grandparents on both the maternal and paternal side who battle addiction, has parents who drink somewhat regularly, and got caught trying alcohol, parents should take additional precautions, such as arranging counseling and deepening supportive, educational conversations in the household. These actions, too, are precautions against disease.

But parents have a responsibility beyond their DNA and the rules they put in place in their homes around drinking. Our children mimic us and can't help but want to emulate our behaviors. Our use of substances, including alcohol, influences our children's relationships with substances. Take that fact and throw it into today's environment, and one can see how an at-risk student can get from zero use to experimenting to residential treatment in months.

Yes, things have changed, and parents play a vital role in helping children navigate the challenging path.

Can a struggling child who quits other substances still drink?

One might be surprised how often I'm asked whether a child struggling with other substances can still drink alcohol. It's a question usually posed by parents of students who have been to treatment or who are struggling to the point that they need treatment.

In cases of children who've been to treatment, the issue is often more about the parents, who don't like to see their children struggle. And what I mean by that is, watching their child decline due to substance abuse was excruciating, because the fact that a young person was in treatment in the first place meant that things had gotten bad. But parents want so much for their children, and one insatiable desire is for their children to be accepted and included among peers. It's hard, if not nearly impossible, for a parent to watch other teens or college students fraternizing while their child is left at home alone. And since alcohol is frequently a key ingredient in student socialization, many parents hope and want to believe that once their child is home from treatment and successfully off harder drugs like cocaine or opiates, they can "learn" to socially drink. These parents don't want their child left out of parties, future weddings, golfing socials, or hunting trips.

It doesn't work that way, however. Most families try to make it work. I'd say that after a young person gets home from an initial residential treatment, the chance is high that either the child will try to persuade their parents that they can still drink or the parents will subconsciously or consciously say to their child, "You can have a beer, right?" I encounter these scenarios routinely, and routinely they go poorly.

The issue is that once a young person has used powerful drugs, including marijuana, cocaine, opiates, or all of the above, their brain changes. Such substances will always have a special place in their brain, which, if awakened, tends to beg and cry out for attention. "All addictive drugs affect brain pathways involving reward—that is, the dopamine system in the reward pathway," according to the University of Utah's Genetic Science Learning Center. "Within seconds to minutes of entering the body, drugs cause dramatic changes to synapses in the brain. By activating the brain's reward circuitry, drugs deliver a jolt of intense pleasure."

Consider how alcohol immediately affects the brain, lowering inhibitions. After drinking considerable amounts of alcohol, many of us have thoughts that wander to the wrong places. With me, for instance, infidelity was an issue. When my inhibitions were reduced and my judgment was impaired, my common sense lost ground, leading to poor decision-making. But when I'm stone-cold sober, infidelity doesn't cross my mind. The formula goes like this: drink too much + introduce craving = trouble. And a person addicted to opiates may face similar substance-induced behaviors.

My son William's experience is an excellent example of this slippery slope in action. He found success and sobriety in treatment, but cocaine and opiates were his weak spot. Once he felt strong after months of sobriety, he thought perhaps he could drink and continue to avoid those other substances. He was living and working in Nashville and wanted to rejoin his college friends out on the town. The first time he drank, it went fine. He could manage the alcohol in that moment. The next time, or the next, he had more, and then his brain unlocked that spot that craved marijuana. Sure, he'd have that. Soon, he'd had that, and he ended up taking cocaine and then cocaine laced with opiates, and he was dead.

I see this more often than one might imagine. Even if the suffering person doesn't end up dead, they may end up in jail, in a fight, or late for work. It just doesn't work to let in some substances while guarding against others. When you suffer from substance use disorder, substances are not your friend. Parents must understand that there's no "beer only" solution that will work, or not for long anyway. Eventually, they'll have more than a few; once that happens, they are likely on the road to nowhere again.

Even for young folks not on the far end of the substance use disorder spectrum, drinking alcohol is problematic. First, yes, there is a spectrum, established by the American Psychiatric Association's *Diagnostic and Statistical Manual of Mental Disorders*, which includes "mild," "moderate," or "severe" substance use disorder, with severe qualifying as addiction. I explain it to students as a one-to-ten scale, with ten being the most intense form of substance use disorder, when someone is on multiple substances multiple times a day—likely opiates and other life-threatening substances. Someone who lands at what we'll call a three on the scale likely has periodic problematic bouts with alcohol or other substances but isn't using daily in life-damaging amounts and may not use daily at all.

A recent college graduate named Ellie, who contacted me by phone after encouragement from her mother, was someone I quickly assessed as a three on my unofficial spectrum. She was not in immediate danger, she was not at high risk, and she struggled primarily with alcohol, though she'd misused prescription or counterfeit prescription pills during binge episodes. Ellie preferred beer and mostly drank beer, unless she was at a nice party where she felt wine might appear more "ladylike." She'd get drunk on beer more often than she liked, she explained, but those bouts of intoxication didn't typically result in a crisis. Maybe she'd send a text she shouldn't have or she'd have to pay for an expensive Uber at peak time after she'd stayed out longer than planned. But her times of trouble—striking her mother after a late-night family tailgate or throwing up on the dinner table at her best friend's rehearsal dinner—came from hard liquor, lots of it.

Ellie explained that on those occasions she had planned to drink only wine or beer. The issue came after multiple wines or beers when the party hit a different gear. Friends purchased shots of liquor she didn't want but also didn't want to turn down, for instance, or someone passed around a jug of homemade margaritas at the tailgate. Those were the times when she was in trouble.

"My mom said you might know what I should do about this," she said.

"What do you think you should do?"

"Quit drinking?" Ellie said quietly, without confidence.

I remained silent.

"Or," she said, "maybe I could just decide to stick with beer. I don't get in trouble when I drink beer, so can't I just do that?"

"I think that's the question," I said. "Can you?"

I know the answer. It's no. Most who land anywhere on the substance use disorder spectrum learn that substances don't benefit their lives, period. Also, alcohol has a way of leading us to do what we don't want, especially for those who can't manage it well. For almost everybody, for instance, alcohol creates a self-inflated view of themselves, leading to risky behavior. Those who struggle with alcohol, even from a lower point in the spectrum, can drink with few repercussions on occasion. It's doable. It's also a time bomb, and when it explodes, the cost damage is high.

That's why some young folks who struggle but can still function don't always get the full parental support they need to stop drinking and make it stick. It's hard, I know, to think about your child living alcohol-free when so many of their peers can't get enough. You have to remember, though, that it's more about your child's health, happiness, and wellbeing than how much time they get with the crowd. Also, there are teens who don't drink or don't want to drink. Many of us, young and old, prefer a clear mind, and we're looking for people like us.

It's essential to know that soon enough your child will be in their midtwenties and the fact that they arrived at that time in their life clear-minded and in charge of themselves will be noticed by friends, hiring managers, and everyone else who encounters them. It will pay high dividends—placing them above the crowd you so eagerly wanted them to rejoin.

What can parents do to delay and reduce alcohol use?

Studies show that alcohol is often the first illegal substance children try, and they often do so at a young age, when they are still heavily under parental and family influence. This means parents have a critical role and responsibility. I'm not saying parents can stop it, because statistically most children will try alcohol by the time they are seniors in high school. The key is working to delay that first taste in order to increase the odds of their wellbeing.

First, it's critical to understand that you are your children's most important role model and they watch almost everything you do. If you reach for a drink daily at 5 PM, they notice. They see if you binge drink at a party and come home tipsy. And they will be more likely to do the same—much more likely.

Even the tiniest of children notice our every move. When my grandson Wilder was two years old, he walked over to a small, glass-fronted drink refrigerator in our home. He started pointing to the drinks he associated with his family, including his parents and grandparents.

"Daddy's drink," Wilder said, pointing to a red Coke can.

Hudson, his father, quit drinking alcohol more than a decade ago and frequently has a soda in his hand when we gather.

"DD's," he said, pointing to a LaCroix to note my drink.

I'm his DD, and I quit drinking years before his birth, so I often have a soda in my hand when we're together.

"Mommy's drink," he said, pointing to an IPA.

His mother doesn't drink much or daily, but he has seen her have a beer occasionally, and has noticed.

"KK's drink," he said, pointing to a chilling bottle of white wine on the bottom rack.

My wife, whom he calls KK, doesn't drink much in terms of quantity but has one glass of wine on many days, and this he has noticed, too.

Our children, or grandchildren, don't miss a single thing we do. That's why I bristle each time the parent of a college student calls me, complaining that their child is addicted to marijuana and they're sick of it. More times than not, the parent is functioning with substance use disorder, drinking high quantities of alcohol, and yet they don't understand why their child is using marijuana daily.

The apple, as they say, doesn't fall far from the tree. If alcohol is a part of your daily or near-daily life, don't expect your children to have a different relationship with alcohol and potentially other substances. So, if you drink, drink responsibly, and take a good, long look at the frequency of your alcohol intake and the importance you place on it when you do consume it.

The other role parents can and should play is having regular, informative discussions with their children about alcohol sooner than one might think necessary. Remember that data shows that many have their first drink at ages eleven or twelve. Especially if your child reaches puberty early, or if other factors like genetics reveal risk is high for your child, don't fear the dialogue. Education has long been among the most significant factors for our choices. And by the time children get to middle school, I can assure you they're hearing and learning about alcohol and other substances. Don't delay the conversation, and don't have it with them just once. Make it routine, discussing regularly why people use alcohol, and its dangers. Also discuss life in general—in particular, happiness and joy and what takes those things away. Avoid centering the conversation on fear and punishment; try not to say things like "If you drink, you'll be grounded for months." While that may be true, that reason alone has never stopped a curious child. Talk about the law, and explain that underage drinking is illegal and can lead to other mistakes, like early sex and sexual assaults. And show empathy and compassion for what children face. Having these honest, engaging conversations can help delay teen drinking by months, if not years. And that delay can significantly affect the rest of their lives.

Parents should look for other risk factors beyond early puberty. Life transitions—including parental separation or divorce, moving, starting a new school, getting cut from a team or tryout when other friends make it, normal puberty, and illness or death within the family—can put a teen on a path to trying a substance or a new substance. In addition, the chances teens will try a substance for the first time increase during idle periods, including the holiday season, summer break, and fall and spring breaks.

It's wise for parents to increase communication with middle, high school, and college students amid life transitions and prior to periods of more idle time, while also monitoring who your child's friends are, what your child's habits are, and how your child and those friends spend time together away from home. Create fun time with your teen or college student that doesn't involve alcohol. I cannot emphasize enough the value of quality family time, even, and perhaps especially, with college students. And engaging your child in discussion about the activities they enjoy to relieve stress—and making your child part of this conversation at an early age and continuing through college—contributes to happy, healthy children and families.

TAKEAWAYS

- The longer a teen waits to drink, and the lower the quantity and frequency of their drinking if they do try alcohol, the greater their odds are of avoiding addiction later on in life.
- Teens who physically mature early are at higher risk of drinking early and thus of facing substance use disorder later.
- Genetics, social circumstances, and environment play vital roles in determining if a child will struggle with substances.
- If your child has struggled with substances, don't believe they can return to "just alcohol." Likely, they can't.
- If you binge drink, your children are more likely to do the same.

6

ANXIETY AND DEPRESSION

The CDC says that one in five children in the United States suffer from a mental health disorder; the most common are attention deficit hyperactivity disorder (ADHD), anxiety, behavior problems, and depression (it's not uncommon for these to occur together). The prevalence of these mental health challenges explains why substance misuse is such a problem for students—when we humans feel pain, we'll reach for the easiest relief. Often, especially for teens, this results in the use of substances as self-medication.

For parents, this poses a question that can't always be answered with immediacy: Which came first, the chicken or the egg? In other words, are substances creating the anxiety and depression, or are the anxiety and depression driving the substance misuse?

Human nature dictates that when we suffer pain, even mild pain or anxiety, we look for the easy means of alleviating that pain. It's that way for youth, adults—all of us. Experiencing more stress at work? Sure, I'll take another splash of wine.

Students face an additional challenge, in that their undeveloped brains can struggle to control emotions and thought processes. They don't naturally have a toolbox from which to draw healthy methods for relieving their pain. And because their ability to clearly and honestly communicate is also often undeveloped, they may struggle to articulate their feelings of depression, shame, and inadequacy—the array of complicated emotional struggles. In addition to these internal struggles, they're also facing messaging in social environments that suggests certain substances can combat negative emotional feelings and provide relief. So when one friend says to another, "Hey, I've got alcohol" (or a pill, or some marijuana, or all of these), it's easy to see how and why someone might choose to use a substance as a means of escape. In this way, mental health and substance misuse converge powerfully.

In students from middle school to high school, I routinely see that some progress has been made in breaking the stigma around mental health (although not so much around the substance use disorder side of it). They feel more comfortable sharing what they face, but it's still only micro progress. Most, for example, will not self-identify with substance struggles or depression, but many will speak up and say, "I battle anxiety."

Anxiety is the safe word for this generation, something they can pinpoint to parents, peers, and others to explain that they don't feel 100 percent right. I'll often ask groups of high school students if anyone struggles with anxiety. In posing the question, I intend to merely get them to think, to respond internally, but routinely three-quarters of the attendees physically raise their hands—yes to anxiety! I stopped asking the question to groups because I don't want to provoke someone into expressing what they may not be ready to share. It helped me learn, however, that the majority struggle with something, as we all do.

And they are anxious—very.

Even for the 50 percent who have so many things going well in their life, having so much can make everything feel like nothing.

A junior in high school, Ginger, explained this predicament:

> I live in a beautiful home with a family that loves me, and I love them so much. We have dinners together and take great trips. I have good grades. I'm going to Disney World next month, and my soccer team just played for the state championship. I have a good church youth group. I have so many nice friends. And when I got my driver's license, my parents got me a car. I have a cute boyfriend; he sends me nice, supportive messages.
>
> But I'm anxious, and frequently depressed. I battle an eating disorder that I keep hidden and I've had suicidal thoughts. I'll tell my mother I'm anxious and she'll say, "You have everything. You are going to Disney next month. Why can't you be excited when many don't have a warm meal at home?" And then I feel worse. I know I should be happy, but I'm not. I can't explain it.

In the several years since puberty, the young lady has battled her eating disorder. She and her friends dabbled together initially—purging, and taking laxatives—but her dabbling went too far, and when she couldn't stop, her weight spiraled downward. At first, she received compliments, which she liked. Then she got troubled stares, which caused her to feel shame, which then deepened the behavior that had brought the glances. Ginger started seeing a psychiatrist who prescribed antianxiety medication, and she regained weight.

However, she told me, she still can't explain precisely what makes her so uneasy.

"I know I have everything," she said. "Sometimes it feels so bad, though."

I asked Ginger what she wanted in life. She said she wasn't sure.

"No, wait. I want to feel good. That's it. I just want to feel good all the time."

That's when I realized what she and so many other teens face, because I hear similar stories so frequently from high school and college students.

I know I have so much, so why do I often feel so bad?

It might make you wonder if many are following a road of others' expectations instead of choosing their daily path. School, soccer, Disney. These activities are what the "have" teens do; they excel in a sport or activity, work hard at school, and take trips. They are nonstop busy—so busy they don't get the chance to reflect or choose a divergent path that might be wholly rewarding for them. Or, as Ginger explained, they're so busy chasing the Instagram moment, in an attempt to prove to others the quality of the life they're living, that they can't stop and actually enjoy the moment.

And then there's the other 50 percent, the have-nots, whose feelings of having nothing going for them are a heavy burden. Poverty in childhood is linked to anxiety, depression, and psychological distress. It can become a self-fulfilling downward spiral, leading to struggles in school, which create more mental health struggles and attract stigma. Their need for role models, engaged learning, and meaningful activities—the things more well-off teens already have—often goes unmet.

MANY COLLEGE STUDENTS ARE LONELY

After high school, something different happens to students, particularly those on the college path. So much of the "go, go, go" structure that can be exhausting—from daily team practice to seven-hour school days and family dinners—goes away overnight with graduation, leaving many uncomfortable with their new spare time, freedom, and isolation. It's everything they've wanted, except for isolation, but the change is drastic. So even when surrounded by everything and everyone in their new life, they can still feel all alone.

A 2017 study by the American College Health Association found that loneliness is so common on college campuses that 67 percent of female students and 54 percent of male students felt "very lonely" in the past twelve months. Social media contributes because "fear of missing out," or "FOMO," is real, causing envy and a lack of self-esteem. College students can look at social media and feel like they're missing out on everything when they're sitting in a dorm room studying while something "fun" is going on somewhere most of the time. And first-generation college students and those with lower economic means often feel less connected to the college scene—they feel more out of place and, therefore, lonelier.

It's a bad feeling for many students, and "very lonely" poses a high risk, since loneliness is painful and, as previously noted, we look for means to alleviate our pain, including substances, unhealthy relationships, overeating, undereating, and overexercising. These negative coping mechanisms only deepen internal struggles even though they may provide short-term distraction.

NATURAL REMEDY

When Clay, a college sophomore, reached out to me late one spring regarding anxiety, depression, and alcohol misuse, with anxiety and depression the most challenging, I referred him to a counselor, and he immediately began therapy. Weeks later, he messaged me to say that he was feeling stuck and needed more help. I'm not a counselor and won't fill that role; I make referrals because counseling works. But it takes time, and it isn't a sort of magic pill or wand. Clay was seeing a counselor weekly, yet the springtime skies were blue and flowers were in bloom and he was stuck in his apartment, depressed and in a rut. I couldn't help but respond.

"You need to start taking a daily walk," I said.

Silence.

"You need to walk," I said. "I know where you live. I walk that neighborhood all the time. It's beautiful out. Start walking. No phone, no music. Just walk every day, smell the flowers, and look into that blue sky. Find yourself."

"I'd feel silly," he said.

"Silly?"

"Girls walk. Guys don't walk."

"Yes, they do. I walk almost every day."

"I mean college guys."

"Activity is a proven boost to mood. Walking, in particular, is easy and meditative, and it's like a drug, improving your mood with increased blood circulation to your brain and body. It's like a super vitamin. The counselor can't do that for you. You've got to do that for yourself. Walk!"

Clay was an honors college student. His father was a physician. Yet I had to explain to him that one of the best medicines for anxiety and depression on a spring day is to just put on tennis shoes, open the door, and start walking. And he was debating this—worrying about how it might look. Thus, it's not just algebra we must teach in middle school. Students must learn about their wellbeing, becoming well equipped to manage themselves when parents aren't around (and even when they are). To get there, more engaged and personalized teaching is required, and it's needed upstream—before students reach college without the needed coping tools.

Clay was shy about taking off on a springtime afternoon walk, feeling like all his peers were watching. He did it, however, and while it wasn't quite like Forrest Gump and running, Clay liked the walking so much he kept going, the sunshine on his face lifting his spirits and the movement increasing the blood flow to his brain and improving his mood. Had Clay refused to add some natural remedy to his counseling, and instead increased marijuana or alcohol intake, his condition would have further deteriorated rather than drastically improving. Yes, counseling is required, but also, we must encourage teens and college students to help themselves by taking a step or steps forward.

That's because nature's remedies can work so well, if we are willing to try them.

HOLISTIC EDUCATION REQUIRED

Jonathan Eckert, a professor and the Copple Chair for Christians in School Leadership at Baylor University, worked in the U.S. Department of Education in both the Bush and Obama administrations, focusing on teaching-quality issues. Eckert says in his book *Just Teaching* that while teaching students holistically seems daunting, it's not impossible. He says that changes are needed to break the mental health and self-medication crisis, and we must provide all students with more individualized care and engagement earlier in the education process. That means middle school and early high school, because studies show that more students become less engaged with each passing year.

Eckert writes, "Holistic, personalized learning is best mediated through deep relationships. Education is more than accruing skills and knowledge for an economic outcome. Through significant educational disruption, we have learned that being present and in relationship matters for each student."

Eckert says that holistic student education is about "the essence of personalized learning—being seen, known, and appreciated as an individual by people who attend to student well-being, student engagement, and provide meaningful feedback for growth."

A report on the 2016 Gallup Student Poll reveals the following findings related to student success and wellbeing:

1. Engaged and hopeful students fare better on desirable outcomes, such as better self-reported academic performance and less absenteeism.
2. Students become less engaged as they journey through school.
3. Many students have a best friend at school, but few get to do what they do best every day.
4. Getting to do what they do best drives high school students' perception of success at school.
5. Many young students but few older students feel surrounded by caring adults at school.

6. Engagement and hope are linked to students' plans after high school.

7. Entrepreneurial aspiration wanes for high school students.

8. Involvement in extracurricular activities boosts positive outcomes for students.

Hope. Engagement. Involvement. A best friend. Time around caring adults. These practices seem to be common sense—they are presumably what every student should be taught and exposed to as tools for fighting back against loneliness, anxiety, and depression. But looking closely at the list, we can easily see how many students can become less engaged as they progress through high school and then experience a big cut in their support systems once they enter their college years, a time with fewer caring adults in their lives, less access to a longtime best friend, and perhaps fewer to no extracurricular activities. They can get stuck, and getting them unstuck can feel challenging. But with the right approach and a little work on their part, they can get back on the road to wellbeing.

TAKEAWAYS

- Students can feel lonely even when surrounded by friends and activities.
- *Anxiety* is a safe word for students that many use to articulate other struggles.
- Students need to be seen, heard, and engaged to find success and wellbeing.

- Activities like walking, running, yoga, or pickup games can deliver immediate, mood-boosting results.
- Students who are suffering from anxiety or depression should find a counselor and keep a counselor.

7

COUNTERFEIT PILLS + FENTANYL

You may think you know this story, but you don't—not the entirety of it and not the severity of it. Counterfeit pills and fentanyl threaten both the lifeblood and stability of millions of individuals and families throughout the country today, tomorrow, and in the coming years. So listen up.

I'll start with an example about a twenty-three-year-old recent college graduate from Texas. His name is Mike, and he played football at a small Division II university. He was from a conservative southern family and attended church most Sundays. His father drank at least a twelve-pack of beer daily, and his mother drank a lot, though she kept the quantity hidden. They never lost their jobs, but the smell of alcohol on their breath was more memorable to the young man than almost anything else in his family. Mike considered himself one of the good guys—"yes ma'am" or "no sir," he'd say with a smile. He got married during his senior year of college, and two years later he and his wife had their first child, Cody. His wife was a nurse, and Mike sold pharmaceuticals. You'd guess that with a college degree and a job at one of the largest drug companies in this country, he'd have had an idea of what was to come.

But he didn't.

I got a call from Mike. I didn't know him or his wife, but she'd read my memoir, *Dear William*, and remembered how I detailed my addiction to prescription Adderall and Vyvanse in the book. She'd found me on social media and messaged me for my number, and he called.

"I'm struggling a little bit with my medicine," Mike said. "I've lost my job, and I'm afraid my wife will leave me if I don't get this cleaned up."

"Medicine?" I asked.

"I've been on a doctor's prescription for Adderall since middle school," he said. "In recent years, I've had a problem—I've been taking all the pills in the first week. We tried locking them up, and I'd promise to do better. But I started buying them on the street a few months ago because I wanted more.

"I started out taking five or six pills daily. Now, I'm at sixteen or seventeen, and it's making me crazy, man, like really crazy."

"These pills look like Adderall?" I asked.

"Yeah, the dealer told me he's getting them off a friend."

"Hmmm. A friend has that many pills?"

Silence.

"Here's what I suspect," I told Mike. "You found a dealer selling counterfeit or fake Adderall pills. That's not Adderall; it's a crudely made stimulant close to meth. Whoever makes those pills is dusting them with a minute amount of fentanyl to make them more addictive. And it's worked. It's clear you already had substance use disorder related to the prescription Adderall misuse and whatever else you were taking. Now, however, you are hooked on opiates."

"They put fentanyl in my medicine?"

"Okay, listen. I'll say it one more time. It's not medicine, and it's fake, counterfeit. Remember those fake Gucci purses that showed up years ago on the New York streets, and folks bought those things and their friends couldn't tell the difference?"

Silence.

"Right, you are too young. Okay—well, that happened. That's what's happening with these counterfeit pills. They look real, but they are not. Then, dusting them with fentanyl makes them irresistible."

My explanation made sense to Mike, who agreed to get help and checked into a thirty-day treatment program the next day. I heard from him later on the other side, and he was sober and doing well. He sounded more confident and grounded, and he explained that my summation of the situation had been correct.

"That wasn't medicine," he said. "That was fake Adderall with fentanyl. It could have killed me, and should have killed me."

I wish Mike's story was rare rather than the norm of what's happening on the illegal drug scene in the United States. Fentanyl is in every community, large and small, in America, and so are counterfeit pills. The two often go hand in hand. And fentanyl has found its way into counterfeit pills as well as into other popular illegal drugs like cocaine, even though they are seemingly opposites—fentanyl is a downer, while cocaine is an upper (drug users compare it to the sweet and salty appeal). What surprised me the most about Mike's story is the state of this country's awareness of such a devastating crisis. Here was a young, professional college graduate, whom we would assume to be a knowledgeable person. His wife was a practicing nurse. Yet he and his wife had no clue about the proliferation of counterfeit pills or fentanyl.

Mike told me they didn't read or watch the news much outside of sports content—"It's fake or too negative," he said. The truth is, though, that the media hasn't quite caught on to what's happening with fentanyl and counterfeit pills, either, beyond baseline reporting. It's the story of this crisis as a whole. It's why parents and educators are so in the dark. Sure, pieces of information get out. One study says street marijuana is so much stronger than in the past that it's more addictive, and it gets some news play; another report says students on spring break in Florida purchased cocaine laced with fentanyl and nearly died. But is the younger generation watching or reading when this issue does get coverage? In any case, the media rarely puts together the puzzle pieces. And so much of the country suffers from political wars and distrust that few trust the news when it is delivered. So here is an overview of what's happening—what every parent, student, and educator must know about the fentanyl crisis, because it's a matter of life and death.

THE RISE OF FENTANYL

You've undoubtedly heard the part of this story about how America got hooked on opiates because Purdue Pharma, privately owned by the Sackler family, had the big idea about making OxyContin, an extended-release oxycodone painkiller that was supposedly safer from addiction. The slow release persuaded the FDA, which approved the drug, and Purdue pushed it across this country as a salve for all pain, even though OxyContin could be easily abused by crushing, snorting, or injecting. Many physicians upped their dosage at Purdue's encouragement, unleashing opioid addiction upon even those unsuspecting patients who were taking it as prescribed. It started in the hills of West Virginia, with pain doctors pushing the pills like revivalists push scripture, but soon spread across the country, with pain pills eventually finding their way into high schools and onto college campuses.

I remember talking to a mother from Iowa in 2012 who explained that in her small town the boy's bathroom at school had become a sort of crack house where students gathered to barter for pain pills that were crushed and snorted between periods. Her son, a tenth grader, got hooked, unaware the pills qualified as illegal drugs. He thought they were "medicine" that made him feel good, the mother explained. Within months, he went from a picture-perfect, front-row, "yes ma'am" student to a child who stole money from his parents and was failing in school.

Once the complex realities of opioid addiction gained attention, demand pressure was applied to the supply chain, targeting pill-pushing doctors. The supply reduction pushed opiate addicts to buy heroin, leading to a resurgence in a drug that for decades had been viewed as the scourge of the street—something only the worst of the worst used, stereotypically while living on the street and using dirty needles. The popularity of less expensive, easier-to-get heroin soared. Meanwhile, this was happening amid other prescription pill pushing that didn't gain much attention at all. Adderall, a stimulant that helps with attention deficit disorder and is often prescribed to students, and Xanax (alprazolam), a drug in the benzodiazepine class that is used to treat anxiety and depression, surged into the market. These drugs and others like them are frequently abused, especially by students. (Let me say that these drugs and others have medical benefits when used as prescribed. We mustn't create shame or stigma around proper use. What we're talking about here is misuse.)

In high schools and on college campuses in particular, the abuse of Adderall and Xanax has soared, along with the widespread misuse of other prescription drugs like Percocet, an opiate. Xanax, a drug that is highly addictive because it creates a euphoric high, became popular for mixed use with alcohol (it greatly intensifies the effects of alcohol) and cocaine, and for helping ease anxiety when coming down from the popular party drug MDMA (Molly).

Those who misuse Xanax for extended periods of time can lose memory—students are so used to this effect that many refer derogatorily to friends with memory loss due to Xanax as "bar-tards," because the often-abused generic version comes in a bar of four pills. As for Adderall, students misuse it to cram for exams or write the paper they procrastinated on the week before, or they use it to party longer on a big day and night of bingeing. Adderall is a stimulant classified as a Schedule II drug by the U.S. Drug Enforcement Administration (DEA), meaning it has a "high potential for abuse, with use potentially leading to severe psychological or physical dependence." When Adderall (which has the opposite effect of Xanax) is taken with alcohol, it works more like cocaine, pushing against alcohol's depressive influence. The idea that the drugs offset one another is only the user's perception, however, as both are hard at work against the body's central nervous system.

Perhaps because drugs like Adderall and Xanax originated from doctors' prescriptions and pharmacies, many teens and college students of this generation don't view them as being as dangerous as street drugs like cocaine. One study revealed that 40 percent of teens view prescription drugs as safer than street drugs and that 25 percent of teens have taken pills not pre-scribed to them. They'll share Adderall and antianxiety pills, or hydrocodone or Percocet if someone gets a prescription and has extras. I've tested this student perception of the relative danger of certain drugs many times in conversations with different sets of teens or college students: I ask questions about how they might feel about consuming a fifth of vodka versus a bottle of Adderall without a prescription, and they routinely say the vodka is worse. And with more than forty million adolescents in America, the result of this kind of thinking is a rise in the popularity of misused prescription pills that has created more demand, outstripping the supply that the medical field pushed into the system. Thus, the increase in the counterfeit pills, standing fraudulently in place of the misused prescription pills and presenting far more danger.

Counterfeit pills look like the real deal to unsuspecting eyes, but if you look closely, there are typically noticeable differences in quality, including discoloration and other inconsistencies. Most counterfeit pills are made by drug lords in foreign coun-tries, including China, Mexico, and India, and then trafficked to the United States, where they are sold to buyers via social media and the mail, and on the street. And production labs in the U.S. are increasing. Regardless of where these pills are made, they are all the more dangerous because they have no quality standards and are made from materials including rat poison, antifreeze, meth, and fentanyl.

Yes, fentanyl. You might wonder why drug lords and deal-ers would put fentanyl—the most addictive, deadly drug on the market—into a counterfeit pill like fake Adderall. It's not that they want to kill the user. Hardly. It's that they have learned that counterfeit Adderall, Xanax, or oxycodone (M30, or "Blues") alone is only so effective at getting the user hooked and coming back for more. But if they splash a minute amount of fentanyl into those pills, the buyers, like Mike, keep coming back again and again. They can make fentanyl, the synthetic opioid that is often 100 times more potent than morphine, inexpensively. Because small amounts are so powerful, they dust it into all the counterfeit pills produced, and presto! The customers keep returning for more and more, unaware of what's happening to them. But with crude production, many counterfeit pills contain lethal amounts of fentanyl. The DEA revealed in 2021 that testing of fake pills showed four out of ten included a lethal dose of fentanyl. Again, it's not that the counterfeit drug producers want to kill their customers. It's that fentanyl is so dangerous that when crude producers get the recipe wrong, it's often enough to kill. Think about baking a cake when you're in a hurry. You quickly mix the ingredients and put the cake in the oven. Later, you take a bite, and it's not bad, but you encounter a clump of flour that didn't get mixed. That's how sloppy counterfeit pills are made—those clumps of fentanyl are deadly. And that's precisely why accidental drug overdoses among young adults in America are soaring.

But it's not just the overdoses creating our crisis. When I'm talking to students, I frequently ask them to tell me about the risks of substance misuse. They'll mumble and stammer, talking about economic loss and becoming addicted, or hurting someone you love, and yes, all of those are correct. But then I tell them the two major risks of substance misuse that I see working with the many students I get to know:

1. Dying (overdoses are soaring)
2. Joining the walking dead (that is, going through the motions of life but being in a perpetual fog)

The death of a child is perhaps the single most horrific thing a parent can experience. I've had that experience, and trust me when I tell you it's as awful as you might imagine. But I must say that before our son William died, substances had turned him into the walking dead. He was shuffling through life in a fog, was hard to talk to at times, and was diminished in his ability to truly and deeply engage. He was living among the walking dead, and too many students today are living that life. Frankly, seeing my son living barely alive for a couple of years was nearly as difficult as burying him. The only difference is that dead is dead—there's no hope of getting him back. With the walking dead, there's nothing but hope because healing is available and it can and will give people back the life they deserve.

FENTANYL KILLS

Edward, a college junior, encountered one of those fentanyl clumps in a counterfeit pill obtained in his college community. As a sophomore, Edward had reached out to me for advice. He'd gotten a DUI and assumed he suffered from substance use disorder, as he'd begun drinking alcohol and smoking marijuana early in high school. Friendly with a big smile, Edward captured a room when he walked into it. He contacted me after his arrest and wanted to visit. We sat together on my porch. He explained how he first tried alcohol in middle school and then got hooked on marijuana in high school, using it both to self-medicate for anxiety and depression and to help get him into the social scene. He had a tender heart, and he spoke in a manner that told me he was in deep.

"I'm guessing you've encountered opiates?" I asked.

127

He nodded.

"You remind me more of my son William than any other student I have talked with," I told Edward.

"Yes sir, yes sir, I know."

Edward went to treatment and was doing well, but recovery is not either/or, as in, you are either using or you are cured. It's a lifetime journey that's more about recovery than sobriety, so sobriety can come and go, especially in the early days. Many students also believe that if they get through treatment and stop using the so-called harder drugs, like opiates, they may apply discipline and simply drink alcohol, or drink alcohol and use marijuana. Eventually, they fall down again and learn the hard way that, no, for most, there's only one way to beat this disease. You pray that the moment they fall doesn't involve a clump of fentanyl.

Edward wasn't so lucky. He was doing well that junior year in many respects, with good grades and a lovely girlfriend. Some nights, he was back at the bar, having fun with friends. He appeared like he could manage himself, so friends who struggled with substances and hadn't been to treatment came back to him as if nothing had happened. He'd make a marijuana buy and the drug dealers, seeing he was in action again, would flood his phone with offers day after day. That's a lot for an addict to ignore. He celebrated his twenty-first birthday, and a day or two later, he and several friends made a Percocet purchase from a drug dealer in his college town. Edward and his friends were microdosing the Percocet, cutting a pill into pieces so each could have a slice. But here's the big problem: it wasn't Percocet; it was counterfeit. And it was laced with fentanyl. Edward got a slice of the pill that contained a clump, but it was so tiny, like grains of sugar embedded in the pill, that he didn't notice. So he took a dose, went to sleep, and never woke up. Goodbye, young soul. Another young person gone too soon—just a bit of fentanyl was all it took.

The following week, a friend called from Texas to tell me she had lost her son to an accidental overdose, and a fentanyl-laced pill was the culprit. Weeks later, I received a similar call. Weeks after that, someone I know lost a son who had purchased cocaine laced with fentanyl. These tragedies keep adding up, but the misuse continues.

That's because you can't scare someone suffering from substance use disorder into stopping. Tell an addict there's extra-potent fentanyl going around and they'll nod in agreement about how bad that is, but when they're alone, they'll go looking for that strong fentanyl or other drugs they crave that may be laced with fentanyl. That's because the drugs have rewired their brains and there's no logic. We can't scare this generation into stopping. We have to educate them earlier, so they can keep their brains from getting rewired to make such deadly decisions.

Fentanyl is so potent and so simple to produce that in the last couple of years it has virtually wiped out heroin, which is barely on the streets anymore. (A product is still sold on the streets as "heroin," but typically it's fentanyl powder.) There's no need for the opiate abusers to chase heroin when fentanyl is fifty to eighty times stronger and no more expensive.

For the drug lords, the logic is similar. To make heroin, they plant and harvest poppies, which is time-consuming and labor-intensive. To make fentanyl, they merely need the chemicals and a small room. Several years ago, the drug lords mostly made fentanyl for fentanyl's sake, providing the opioid addicts a powerful, affordable fix. Then they cut it into cocaine, and immediately cocaine sales soared. Then the counterfeit pill market expanded, and they dusted the pills with fentanyl, and those sales exploded, too—boom!

"What we are seeing now is a problem with school-age kids buying a drug commonly referred to as Xanax," said Portland police commander Art Nakamura of the Drug and Vice Division in 2019 on a departmental podcast. "However, none of the Xanax that we are seeing on the street is actually Xanax. We've got pills that contain fentanyl, other synthetics, such as U-4700, which is so new, it doesn't have a name, yet it has a number. These kids don't know what they're buying. There is an incident in the news where there were multiple kids who purchased Xanax from another student and they all overdosed."

When the COVID-19 pandemic struck, drug sales moved almost exclusively online, particularly for teens and college students. The sale of counterfeit pills and fentanyl expanded rapidly, yielding an unimaginable crisis striking tiny towns to big cities across America. It's happening so fast and moving into all areas of the country. Neither parents nor law enforcement officials are prepared to deal with the challenges of counterfeit pills. Consider that in 2021 the DEA alone confiscated more than 20 million fake pills laced with fentanyl—more than in the previous two years combined. The problem is enormous and widespread.

HOW DO YOU DIE FROM FENTANYL?

A side effect of opioids is respiratory depression. Fentanyl is fast acting; the drug interacts with opioid receptors in the brain and spinal cord to keep the brain from getting "pain messages" while delivering feelings of euphoria. These feelings make the person under the influence of fentanyl want more of it, because it wears off rather quickly. To remain "high," they need more and more of the drug, and that's where the side effect of respiratory depression becomes the deadly factor. Opioids block the brain's ability to remember to breathe, resulting in death.

This side effect is scary. However, even for students who are involved in illegal drug use but aren't suffering from substance use disorder, scare tactics are unlikely to work. I recall some college students telling me about a police officer who came to their fraternity house to try to scare them off fentanyl after a friend died from an overdose. They shed all kind of tears for the loss of their friend but wanted to kick that cop's butt right out of the house, because when you try to scare a student, you are talking down to them and insulting them, and they want no part of it. The research says that such tactics don't work, and parents already know this is true from experience. Tell your child the cliff is dangerous, turn your back, and hear the splash. It's not how they are wired. Their young brains can't calculate danger and death like an adult brain can. But we know that education works. We've got to begin the conversations earlier. Young people need to learn that prescription pills and counterfeit pills are increasingly dangerous, and that they will take their joy and keep it, for good.

POPULAR COUNTERFEIT DRUGS INTERNET SEARCH QUESTIONS

(*Source: DEA*)

What are fake or counterfeit drugs?

Counterfeit pills are fake medications that have different ingredients than the actual medication. They could have a little bit of the real ingredients, or none at all. Users won't be able to tell if a pill is real or fake by just looking at it. And, unfortunately, many counterfeit pills contain deadly amounts of fentanyl or methamphetamine.

How can you tell if drugs are fake?

A lot of counterfeit pills are made to appear legitimate. So, there really isn't a clear way to tell if a pill is fake just by looking at it.

What does "laced" mean?

When you hear someone say something is "laced," they mean that a substance was added to it that was not originally there. Examples: Many counterfeit pills are laced with fentanyl. Some snacks are laced with THC (marijuana) oil.

What can fake drugs do?

Since counterfeit drugs are unregulated and made illegally, they can actually be deadly. Just a tiny bit of fentanyl can lead to an overdose, and counterfeit pills often have varying amounts.

FENTANYL TAKES AMERICA

It's intimidating to think about every community in America, big and small, being inundated with counterfeit pills made with rat poison and other dangerous chemicals and often laced with deadly fentanyl. I once told a group who had just lost a friend (a student I had helped) to counterfeit pill/fentanyl overdose that the situation had deteriorated to the point that it felt like true evil personified.

"Growing up," I explained, "my parents took me to church most Sundays, and it was a hellfire, brimstone sermon that both scared me and perplexed me. I didn't want to burn in hell, but I couldn't quite buy into this devil man with a pitchfork. Now, though, I have met the devil. It's fentanyl, and fentanyl in counterfeit pills. It's coming for us, and we've got to fight back."

Yes, we must fight back. We don't have a choice. Today, it's one child lost. Tomorrow, it will be ten children lost at once—a quarter of a sports team or the drum line of a band—the tragedy of friends experimenting together and getting a bad dose.

But we are in the early days of this devastating trend. The mental health crisis is only intensifying. The counterfeit pills are multiplying fast. Fentanyl is deeply embedded in every community and multiplying in volume faster than federal and local agents can stop it. We must fight back, and doing so starts with parents and educators, who are vital members of the student ecosystem. I desperately wish we could diminish the supply, but that's beyond our control. Educating our children is not.

Unfortunately, there's a powerful combination of fentanyl players flooding the deadly, highly addictive drug into the U.S. from international illegal drug lords and producers. In 2019 and earlier, for example, most fentanyl arrived in the U.S. from China via mail. Now the supply chain has greatly expanded, with Mexico more deeply involved in producing meth and fentanyl, using chemicals provided by China and India. The flow of fentanyl into the U.S. now comes from "new source countries and new transit countries" compared to when the crisis first emerged in 2014, the DEA said in a 2022 intelligence report. The DEA points out that this exacerbates the already multi-faceted fentanyl crisis, since multiple international parties are now involved in "the global supply chain of fentanyl, fentanyl-related substances, and fentanyl precursors." In other words, nearly a decade ago there were fewer players involved in the fentanyl supply chain. Still, law enforcement couldn't stop it. But the activity was a fraction of what it is today because demand in this country for the potent fentanyl has soared. And the demand in this country has fueled supply.

"There was a change in consumption, there was a change in drug markets due to the ease of producing synthetic drugs," said Mexico's defense secretary, General Luis Cresencio Sandoval, in 2021, noting that drug lords were shifting operations from growing poppies for heroin to running fentanyl production labs.

Governments in China and Mexico aren't much help, either. "China-Mexico law enforcement cooperation against the trafficking of fentanyl and precursor agents for meth and synthetic opioids remains minimal," according to a 2022 report from the Brookings Institution. "China rejects co-responsibility and emphasizes that controls and enforcement are matters for Mexico's customs authorities and other Mexican law enforcement to address. China has maintained this posture even as the presence of Chinese criminal actors in Mexico, including in money laundering and illicit value transfers (which are increasingly featuring barter of wildlife products for synthetic drug precursors), is expanding rapidly."

Translation: There's poison all over this country, and that's not changing any time soon. Since the supply keeps coming, we must work to lessen the demand—a daunting task. But education has been a backbone of this country since its founding, and we must get upstream to reach out to our children and provide them the information they need to navigate these new, treacherous landscapes.

COUNTERFEIT PILL/FENTANYL TIPS

- Beginning in middle school, educate children about the relationship between mental health and substance misuse.
- Provide early education about the life-threatening dangers related to misuse of prescription pills and the distinct differences between prescription and counterfeit drugs.
- Involve teens and college students in the conversation about how they feel or what they know about fake pills and dealer tricks like using fentanyl to make them more addictive.
- Involve your children in conversations about how fentanyl kills and how it also steals joy.
- Humanize the misuse of fentanyl and counterfeit drugs by sharing stories of others your children may know, or who are like them, and how these drugs harmed those people.
- Learn and share about treatment and recovery, so your children know what's likely ahead (besides an increased risk of death) if they use a powerful opioid like fentanyl.
- If you are concerned that your children are

struggling with opiates or other drugs, let them know in an empathetic voice that immediate help is available.

Efforts to educate students beginning in middle school and into college about counterfeit pills and fentanyl start with parents and involve educators, too—school is no longer just about what math class to take, what sport to play, and what language to study. We must put students first and stop fighting among ourselves and pointing fingers on this issue. We can't sit around the dinner table or show up in schools and try to scare students away from counterfeit pills and fentanyl. It doesn't work. That's because once someone suffering from substance use disorder uses fentanyl, intentionally or not, they are no longer able to think clearly. Their mind has been reprogrammed to want relief from pain via drugs. They are already in a substance misuse pattern with alcohol, marijuana, cocaine, and/or prescription or counterfeit drugs like Adderall and Xanax. Nobody sets out to get hooked on a powerful opiate. Most end up there by mistake—through exposure to it via technology and social media, or through efforts to combat anxiety and depression. We need to reduce the number of substance misuse and mental health crises to affect the fentanyl demand.

Yes, America, we have a problem that starts with our mental health and our self-medication obsession, and it's opened the floodgates for fentanyl in this country.

If the DEA and law enforcement can't stop the flow, we must get to our children before it's too late, teaching them about the devil that's trying to steal and keep their happiness and joy or, worse than that, take their last breath.

TAKEAWAYS

- Many teens view pharmaceutical pills taken without a prescription as less dangerous than illegal drugs.
- Prescription pills are more expensive and more challenging to get than fake or counterfeit drugs, which are easily available in every community in the U.S.
- Counterfeit pills are dangerous because they contain chemicals including rat poison and other materials unsuitable for ingestion by humans. They are life-threatening because many—not all, but many—have minute amounts of fentanyl added to make them more addictive.
- Heroin is mostly gone from the streets in the U.S. The product dealers label as heroin is now usually fentanyl powder.

8

HOW TO KNOW IF TREATMENT IS NEEDED

Breaking the stigma in our culture surrounding addiction and those who receive treatment is a significant challenge, but breaking that stigma among parents, especially in relation to their own children, presents an even greater challenge.

Parents are often just as afraid, or even more afraid, of how their child might be labeled as their child is. Consider that the first thing most parents say out loud at the initial suggestion that their teen or college student needs treatment is "Do others have to know?"

That's not the only fear either. Parents worry about interrupting their child's life and routine because it will get them out of pace with peers, whom they perceive as steadily moving along the success track. Never mind that treatment for someone suffering from substance use disorder is the key to success in their life. But let's pause this discussion about taking that bold and necessary step of getting a child into treatment and look first at the number one question parents from throughout the country consistently ask me: "How do we know if our child needs substance treatment?"

Let's establish this from the outset: Odds are exceptionally high that your child cannot identify the scope of their suffering, much less diagnose themselves with a disease like addiction. Most who suffer don't fully begin to understand how significantly they were struggling until they are weeks into sobriety. When we help people who are in denial about the depth and impact of their substance abuse get into treatment, they often don't see the reality of their condition until about the third week. This delay between needing help and realizing help is needed can prevent parents from getting a clear picture of their child's situation when they approach their child about it. When parents notice alarming changes in their child's behavior, they often sit down with their child—concerned, if not angry—and ask questions to which the child responds with answers that feel like the truth but are in fact just a shadow of the truth, because the child cannot fully understand the extent of their suffering.

Most of us are ashamed of our substance use, so fully admitting it to others, much less to ourselves, doesn't come easily, especially on the first try. Also, the substances we get hooked on trick our minds into thinking we need them, so we'll try almost any tactic to avoid having them taken away. Thus, an effective assessment of whether your child needs professional help doesn't usually come through parent and child negotiation. Typically, it begins with parents noticing signs and having nonblaming discussions with their child that can provide some hints as to what the problem could be, which then leads to professional assessment. And it's that professional assessment that should help determine if your child needs substance treatment or not.

But before we get into the signs of substance use disorder and other things to know about treatment involving a teen or college student, I'd like to stress the importance of involving a professional who is a substance misuse specialist in this assessment. I bring this up because sometimes I see an individual in counseling with an effective and competent counselor who is not a substance professional, and it can take the individual much longer to get around to the reality that substance misuse is a significant factor in the individual's life.

It's often true that someone suffering from substance misuse has underlying issues of anxiety or depression and they are self-medicating, but to effectively treat those issues, the substances must be removed from the equation. That's because heavy substance use can cause or exacerbate anxiety and depression and other mental health issues and also because treating underlying issues isn't possible with so much substance misuse layered on top. And as previously established, the longer a young person is misusing substances, the greater the odds that they'll battle such behavior later in life. So I tell parents to follow their instincts. Parents know their children best, and if warning signs are flashing or you have feelings of unease—the universal parental "I don't have a good feeling"—trust that you know best. Something is wrong. And that moment, and not a moment later, is time for a parent-child discussion leading to professional assessment.

The signs of substance misuse disorder are outlined later in this chapter in the box "Defining Substance Use Disorder and Addiction," and it's also critical to pay close attention to verbalized cues your teen or college student may give that we identify as "change talk." Remember, we humans and especially younger humans have a difficult time making blunt statements like "I need help." Typically, parents aren't prepared to notice when that's what their children are saying, only in different words. Often this change talk will be something like "I don't like my roommates; I want to move out and get a fresh start," or "The professors don't like me here; I need to try a new school."

In other words, your child may blame the context for their problems, which is very common. They may be subtly crying out for help, however, and your conversations with them can help guide them to that recognition. The best approach here is to apply the "Five Whys" technique of questioning, which is used to uncover the cause and effect of an underlying problem.

An example:

"The professors don't like me here; I need to try a new school."
Why question 1: "Why don't the professors like you?"
"They don't like that I turn my work in late, but in high school it didn't matter."
Why question 2: "Why do you turn your work in late?"
"Because I'm tired all the time so it's taking me longer."
Why question 3: "Why are you tired all the time?"
"Because I'm the rush chairman for my fraternity, and I have to take rushees out every night and get them drunk, and I have to drink too much also."
Why question 4: "Why do you have to drink too much with the rushees?"
"I don't have to. I plan not to but always end up doing that."
Why question 5: "Why do you end up doing that?"
"I don't know, maybe I have a problem."

At this point, the moment is perfect to strongly suggest your child get an assessment to determine what level of counseling or care may be needed. If your discussions don't have such fruitful results, getting professional assessment is the best and only option as a next step. Remember, your parental instinct is rarely wrong, and your children rely upon your structure and guidance to help get them on the right track. You don't want to accuse them, but you do want to get them into assessment if the warning signs are there. Let's look first at the definition of substance use disorder (see box), then we'll discuss the options for treatment, and finally we'll examine some of the best steps to take after treatment.

DEFINING SUBSTANCE USE DISORDER AND ADDICTION

(*Source: Partnership to End Addiction*)

What Is Substance Use Disorder?

Substance use disorder, which has also been referred to as abuse, dependence, and addiction, is diagnosed if certain criteria occur within a 12-month period as defined by the DSM-5 (the *Diagnostic and Statistical Manual of Mental Disorders* from the American Psychiatric Association).
The criteria include:

1. The substance is often taken in larger amounts or over a longer period than was intended.

2. There is a persistent desire or unsuccessful effort to cut down or control use of the substance.

3. A great deal of time is spent to obtain, consume, and recover from a substance.

4. Craving, or a strong desire or urge to use the substance, occurs.

5. Continued use of the substance results in a failure to fulfill major role responsibilities at work, school, or home.

6. Use of the substance is contributing to relationship problems.

7. Important social, occupational, or recreational activities are given up or reduced because of use of the substance.

8. Use of the substance is recurrent in situations in which it is physically hazardous (e.g., driving while intoxicated).

9. Continuing to use the substance despite knowing that it has an impact on physical or psychological problems likely caused by the substance (e.g., drinking with a liver condition or using opioids when depressed or anxious).

10. Tolerance, which means that the person needs more of a substance to get a desired effect or the same amount of a substance doesn't produce the desired effect any longer.

11. Withdrawal, such that when the substance is not taken, a person experiences substance-specific withdrawal symptoms.

You'll note that the *DSM* does not specify a certain amount like a six-pack of beer or two joints a day, but rather focuses on the lack of control, significant relationship and social problems, risky use, tolerance, and withdrawal symptoms. People who meet two or three criteria are considered to have a "mild" disorder, four or five is considered "moderate," and six or more symptoms is "severe." Many people experience substance use problems but are able to stop using or change their pattern of use without progressing to addiction.

What Is Addiction?

While the term "addiction" does not appear in the *DSM*, it is generally regarded as a severe substance use disorder. Addiction is the most severe form of a full spectrum of substance use disorders. It is a medical illness caused by repeated misuse of a substance or substances.

Addiction is defined by the National Institute on Drug Abuse (NIDA) as a chronic disorder characterized by compulsive drug seeking, continued use despite harmful consequences, and can result in long-lasting changes in the brain. It's more complicated than other diseases, as it's considered both a complex brain disorder and a mental illness.

WHAT ARE THE OPTIONS
IF MY CHILD NEEDS HELP?

Typically, there are three primary options involving different levels of substance treatment—counseling, intensive outpatient programs, and residential programs—and the best one depends on whether your child is experiencing the "mild," "moderate," or "severe" stage. If their substance use disorder is mild, counseling is likely a good starting point, and let me strongly suggest once again that if you can find a therapist who specializes in substance issues, that will be best. Most communities that are moderately sized or larger have them. In smaller communities, finding a substance misuse specialist might prove challenging, but it's worth the extra effort to search for someone with this specific expertise. If assessment suggests your child's substance misuse is moderate, then counseling, support groups, and/or intensive outpatient programs (IOPs) are likely required. IOPs are excellent options for young people, and they work very well, even if as a first step in the assessment process. What I mean is that by attending an IOP in their community, at home, or in college, they can remain in their environment while getting significant treatment, surrounded by others facing similar challenges. IOPs typically provide the same treatment as residential facilities; the one big difference is that the client continues to live in their home and participate in their usual activities. IOPs are most effective as a first treatment option, and often this is enough. For my son Hudson, for instance, and many, many other young men and women I know, one thirty-day IOP experience kick-started their sobriety journey enough to lead to years of recovery. Also, IOPs are effective for step-down—the follow-up option after residential treatment. For some, though, the IOP gets them started on the journey and they learn during the process that residential treatment is needed. That doesn't mean these people are failures. It means they need residential treatment that takes them out of their environment, and starting with an IOP helps them figure out the next best step.

Those assessed as being in the severe category often move directly into residential treatment. Time is of the essence in these cases, and if people are involved in opiates, as is often the case with severe diagnoses, getting into a different environment quickly can save their lives and spark sobriety and recovery.

It's not unusual for students to resist treatment after assessment, however. Many will deny, deny, deny, despite the evidence. Just let me say this as a reminder: My son Hudson didn't initially want to enter an intensive outpatient program although he had nearly died at a fraternity house on a college campus from an accidental overdose. And the majority of students I help get to treatment don't initially want to go or think they need to go. It's not an unusual reaction, because most who have misused substances have struggled to recognize the problem since they see others around them using more, and also because they can easily contextualize or rationalize misuse.

> I drank so much last Friday because it was the night before the biggest football game.
> I started using cocaine to help me with school because I had trouble waking up for classes.
> I just smoke marijuana daily because I get bored.
> I don't do as much as my friends do.

You will get your child into treatment in one of four ways:

1. **Agreement.** They admit they have a problem and want to go. You make the call immediately and they go within the next day or two.
2. **Bargaining or leverage.** They don't want to go, but you try to entice them—"We're taking your car away unless you go," or "We aren't giving you any money at college unless you get to treatment."
3. **Intervention.** Family and/or friends confront them, demanding they go to treatment. Note: This approach isn't always successful and can result in relational damage given that family and friends aren't experienced professionals trained to deal with such a heavy topic. Increasingly, if this approach is used, family or friends will hire a professional interventionist, who is available in most communities.
4. **Court order.** If they are an immediate danger to themselves or others, a judge can order them to receive treatment in most states.

NAVIGATING TREATMENT OPTIONS AND MANAGING AFTER TREATMENT

For parents, two of the most challenging aspects of getting a child into treatment are the discussion—it's uncomfortable approaching difficult subjects—and the decision about where to send their child for treatment. The good news is that there are many good IOPs and residential treatment facilities throughout the country. The less-than-good news is that there are many not-so-good IOPs and residential treatment centers throughout the country. Ask a trusted professional for advice, and then if you know others in your community who have used recommended facilities, ask for feedback.

Cost is also a significant factor, of course. Treatment is expensive and insurance doesn't usually pay for all of it. And sometimes, a child isn't covered by insurance, limiting treatment options. What I tell parents is to take a deep breath and keep your options open. The location of a facility is less important than it being a good fit, in terms of both its treatment style and expertise and its affordability and accessibility. As for cost, if your child is insured and the insurance company will pay, you have an excellent chance of getting into the facility desired. The treatment facility will expect you to contribute to the portion insurance won't cover, but often this is negotiable. Don't be shy about explaining clearly and honestly what you can pay and what you cannot pay as your portion.

Don't blow your entire savings on the initial thirty-day treatment visit either. That's because for most individuals struggling with severe substance use disorder, it often takes seven or eight days for the treatment to start to stick; it's not always precisely thirty days until they're home and done. I know that might sound intimidating, but checking into treatment the first time is only the beginning, just as finishing the first thirty days is only a first step. Particularly if opiates and other stronger drugs like cocaine are involved, it's unlikely you'll send a child off for thirty days and they'll come back good as new. Eventually, they will be better than ever before, but it's a process. Sobriety is a start. It's the recovery that changes lives. Getting sober means getting a clear mind to allow emotional development to occur—the emotional development that helps us find grounding and peace without substances. The emotional healing and growth that happens near the onset of sobriety takes time; it doesn't happen overnight or in thirty days.

We foolishly believed when checking our son William into his first treatment that he'd get sober, come home, and resume life. We didn't understand that he'd be closer to the average, needing five or six thirty-day sessions before the treatment began to stick. With our son Hudson, thirty days in an intensive outpatient program was enough to get him started on the road to recovery, but it was still just the beginning of his journey. Hudson's success was due in part to finding roommates early on who supported his journey so he didn't feel like an alien.

Within an hour of my writing this portion of the book, I met with a student I've followed since he went to treatment in high school. Marcus went to treatment during his senior year, leaving a prominent private school in Atlanta for an adolescent treatment program because his parents made him do so. In his mind, he knew sobriety was necessary. But his heart wasn't there yet, and so he got ninety days of treatment but thought he could drink alcohol and smoke marijuana without resorting to opiates. Within weeks, however, he was back to opiates and in another treatment facility. It went this way for two years— quick relapse once out of treatment. I feared I'd get a call any day that he'd overdosed.

Marcus's parents suffered every blow, and you could see the deepening lines pain had carved in their brows, but they never gave up—on themselves or their son. He's an only child, and their marriage was strained, but they got counseling and attended Al-Anon meetings separately.

The dreaded call never came, and I'm writing this after spending a fantastic hour with Marcus. I saw a year of recovery in his eyes, and he smiled and told stories of what's he's doing today and what he will do tomorrow. He was strong, warm, and compassionate, reminding me of why I do this work. I have never been so proud of anyone, and I feel that sense of pride every time I see a young person latch onto sobriety and then recover. It's a father's pride, like what I have for my son Hudson. I asked Marcus his secret—what finally worked?

"Sober living," he said—a similar story I hear from other students. The treatment was valuable, integral, he said, of course. The support from twelve-step meetings was vital, he said.

"The difference maker for me was the guys in sober living. We picked each other up and decided we could do this. Everything else was necessary, but sober living was the key piece I didn't have before."

The day I met up with Marcus, he'd just moved into an apartment with three others—only one of them sober. "I can do it," he said, "but it's not easy."

No, it's not easy. Marcus explained that within his first hours back in town, he'd walked into an apartment of friends smoking marijuana. "You don't mind?" they said.

"I don't mind what you do," he said, "but I can't be around it."

"It's not that they don't care about me and what I face," Marcus told me. "They don't understand because sitting around the apartment and smoking marijuana is normal to them."

I reached out to Marcus's father after we met, sharing how proud and impressed I was. His father broke down, sobbing beautiful tears.

"I've got my son back," he said. "I didn't know if we'd get here."

"But here you are. Here he is."

Indeed, the journey is not easy, for anyone. It often takes

longer than expected, requiring intensive work for the student, the family (a vital support agent for change), and even friends. The reward, though, is joyful beyond anything we can experience in this life.

SUBSTANCE TREATMENT SAVES AND CHANGES LIVES

Many parents can't help but resist the idea of sending their child to residential substance or mental health treatment, even though they know better, because they fear the stigma or labeling their child might face. The fact is that those parents' fears are often unfounded, and, if anything, in this era employers and friends love investing time and money in those who have been to treatment and found recovery.

I tell people all the time that if you have three job candidates and everything is equal but one has revealed they are years into successful recovery, hire that person immediately. They have been through so much self-searching and shown such self-compassion and awareness that their emotional intelligence is exceptionally high and they will be A-plus employees. Sure, there's always the risk that someone in long-term recovery might relapse, but the risk that any other employee might fall into substance abuse is no different.

I'd bet on the person in recovery every time, and we're seeing that trend play out in business. The secret is out, and you'll find as you pay more attention that many exceptional entrepreneurs and humans in general are in recovery. Some wear it on their sleeve and others keep it close, but they are there, as powerhouses in your community. So don't believe that voice in your brain for one minute—if your child needs help, act immediately on their behalf and give them a chance to reclaim their best self.

The decision to offer them help despite short-term life interruptions, like leaving school, is the first and most important step. I've watched many parents and spouses experience deep anguish over how to get a loved one into treatment, only to find intense relief and satisfaction once they are there. It's never as difficult as we convince ourselves to bring them to treatment with love and concern once we have the right conversations. It's about taking the first step with meaningful, caring dialogue and walking them through to the answer rather than shoving it upon them. Most humans want joy, and they'll fight for that joy. It's just that once the substances have hijacked a brain, they don't easily let go.

Nobody ever said parenting would be easy, either. Helping your child get support and care can be challenging and complicated, but the relief and hope of getting them to treatment are worth the effort. Don't give up. It's a journey—it works and powerfully changes and saves lives. But like most of us, you will learn that your initial anxiety about getting them to treatment, and into the right treatment, isn't the big challenge at all. Not even close. Our hardest work as parents of children in recovery begins the moment they get out of treatment and come home. This is a challenging part of the journey that's often overlooked.

I've seen too many well-intentioned parents create harm due to this blind spot. Yes, they took action and got their child to treatment. But once their child is home, they offer love and support but don't understand how difficult it is for their child to return home after several months in treatment and watch the family cocktail hour.

During football season, the family attends the tailgate, and liquor flows.

It's Thanksgiving; the extended family is over for the celebration; and wine, beer, and liquor flow throughout the day.

The sober child tells everyone they are fine, that it's okay—because the last thing they want is to become any more of a burden. They feel they've caused enough pain. Their substance use disorder caused months, if not years, of family turmoil and pain, and they are still making peace with their guilt.

I've never seen anything inflict family pain like an addiction. You probably have not either. Children who are otherwise trustworthy will steal money from their mother's purse and a credit card from a sibling to fund their addiction. This behavior reflects the disease, of course, not the child, but that disease does a tornado of damage before they get to treatment. Once released, the child is more apt to sit quietly in a corner while the family drinks through its dinners and celebrations, because they can't stand being a disruption once again.

"I'm fine," they'll say, even as the drinks keep pouring.

A couple of students have explained to me how they relapsed immediately due to this dynamic, not with alcohol but with pills. They wanted to stay sober or maintain the illusion of sobriety so as not to disrupt the party. So they purchased painkillers and appeared sober, even when they weren't. Both have since died of an overdose. And it's not their parents' fault any more than it's my fault that my son William is gone. But we must share what students who've struggled tell us in order to help others. And often, families' behavior comes from the best intentions. Families are under considerable duress when one child or more suffers from addiction and goes to treatment. Parents want to put the family back together again as it was. And they don't know what they don't know. Alcohol is so deeply embedded in our culture that many don't know how to gather without it, nor do they understand its impact on others, especially a young person just out of treatment. I'm not blaming the parents at all. It's just that I can't write this book without speaking the truth, to support all the students who come out of treatment and need their families to understand. Also, I know every parent, every family, wants to understand. They want to know so they can help.

Well, this is how: a child newly in recovery needs you to stand with them, side by side, with all substances, including alcohol, out of the picture.

Does that mean you must give up alcohol forever when you don't have a problem? No, not at all. It's more important in the early days, when sobriety is so fragile, the days when sobriety is in place but recovery is just beginning. Only deep in recovery can an individual find the strength to endure such parties, as the odd person out, sitting with their feelings while everyone else is altering theirs.

Even then, it's rarely easy. I recall a recent holiday when my family gathered and I was deep into recovery, happier than ever before and far removed from substances and the thought of substances. We were sitting around the dinner table and I had a Diet Coke, but three others at the table drank one glass of wine, then a second. It was Christmas Eve and I remembered how an excellent red wine rolls down so smoothly when paired with medium-rare prime rib and Amy Grant songs shimmering in the background. I understood completely that they deserved to enjoy every bit of that moment. And I had the tools to withstand my desire for a glass of wine. I cannot deny, however, how it consumed my thoughts. It wasn't that I desperately wanted a drink, but rather that I desperately didn't like the reminder throughout the dinner that I couldn't drink.

The problem was mine, not theirs, but that's what we face with this disease, and it's much easier to stare moments like that down once you are long into recovery than it is in the early days. So, when I speak this truth—about meeting your child where they are if they come home from treatment—I hope you hear and understand what I am saying and why. It's not to impinge on your habits or assign blame. It's about saving your child's joy, and possibly their life, as it can make all the difference in their success and in your family's future. And the truth is, anecdotal evidence and plenty of research show that parental alcohol misuse can affect teens significantly. Consider that the CDC says that almost 17 percent of U.S. adults binge drink (five or more drinks on an occasion for men or four or more drinks on an occasion for women) and 25 percent do so at least weekly.

The substance misuse crisis knows no economic, social, or cultural boundaries. It touches every family, church, community, and school at some level. If you think addiction won't strike your family, you might get a harsh surprise.

It's true, though, that many families will be spared from actually sending a loved one to treatment. That's because statistically some 10 percent of the population suffers from addiction, the far end of the substance use disorder spectrum, but annually less than 1 percent of that group gets treatment. We've got to do better and see to it that more individuals who need treatment get there earlier. That's why I've written this book and done this work and so many others are leading similar efforts. More individuals need help, but we've got to break the stigma and educate both children and adults about how early treatment changes and saves lives.

Family and friends can enhance the long-term success rate of those fortunate enough to get into treatment by providing support, understanding, and empathy, particularly upon their release. It has everything to do with whether they turn their new sobriety into long-term recovery or fall back into old, dangerous patterns, putting their life at risk.

The family has already suffered significant distress by the time a child or sibling enters treatment. When one family member suffers a mental health issue or substance use disorder, the entire family suffers. Relationships are strained and damaged, and each family member is affected differently yet profoundly. That's because addiction is a disease and therefore takes priority over the person it inhabits, disrupting almost every aspect of their life—relationships, money, morals. Parents will say, "I can't believe my child would do that to me," and I have to remind them that the disease is in charge of what their sweet child wants and their child deserves to get free.

FIGHTING BACK

Addiction drives good people to do bad things, and the list of collateral damage that someone with an addiction creates is typically long. They've likely lied to family, taken money, incurred costs, created legal problems, caused or stoked distrust among family and friends, taken attention and resources away from others, and perhaps even resorted to violence. Each of these actions is a warning sign that someone suffering from addiction is reaching the need-for-treatment stage. And each or all may occur by the time someone gets help and begins healing.

The strain on parents and family is difficult to quantify, as only those who have been through it understand. For the parents, it's a marriage nuclear bomb. Few things drive a wedge between parents like a child struggling with addiction. There are disagreements regarding the problem and its severity, disagreements about the correct remedy, defenses of the child, barriers built up between other children or family members affected by the disruption, and money issues. Addiction is costly—in terms of both emotional suffering and treatment expenses.

Parents must understand that they are on the same team, not at odds with each other, and that counseling and support group meetings are not only helpful but practically mandatory for those on this journey.

I encourage parents to join support groups or begin counseling while their child is away at treatment if they have not already. It's an excellent time to reset, reflect, and learn from the past while aiming toward the future. Under the duress of dealing with a child or children in distress, many parents self-medicate or seek short-term pain relief via less-than-healthy means. A healthy family is strong at the core, which starts with a parent, parents, or guardian. Getting back to the basics of good modeling, especially for key healthy behavior areas such as sleep, physical activity, and a nutritional diet, can set the tone for moving forward in a supportive way.

Remember that because addiction is a family disease, it's not uncommon for more than one family member to have misuse issues. Four in my family were involved at once—me and my two sons (we all suffered from addiction) and my daughter (she had an eating disorder). Everyone's healing can occur in step; often when a child enters treatment and the family works in support, one or both parents recognize their own struggle with substances or other challenges and make life-changing decisions. It's also quite common for siblings to follow a similar path with misuse, and it's not unusual for them to each find recovery—family is our most significant role model.

TAKEAWAYS

- Substance use disorder is a spectrum, and the type of help your child needs depends upon whether their SUD is mild, moderate, or severe (addiction).
- Your child won't know if they need treatment. Those struggling can't easily self-assess. If warning signs exist, seek professional assessment.
- Treatment works, though it can take time. Thirty days is only the beginning. Don't delay; the sooner, the better, to get your child on the road to wellbeing.
- The support your child receives after treatment at home matters. Ask them how you can help.
- Remember that treatment is a beginning. Recovery takes time. Don't expect overnight results.
- Don't expect your child to return to life as it was once out of treatment. Their life will change drastically, but for the better. Your emotional support as they make changes matters a lot.

9

STRONG AT THE CORE

Regarding student mental health and substance misuse, few things matter more than family.

We parents deserve neither all the blame for children who struggle nor all the praise for those who thrive. They get our DNA, the "nature," which affects personality and behavior, including mental health and substance misuse. But that's beyond our control except for the education, awareness, and support we can provide to help manage these issues. Then there's the socialization, the "nurture," which we have more control over since the family is a principal agent in human socialization. This process begins in our early years and includes parents, siblings, and even grandparents if they are involved in a child's life, and it's how we first learn love, and often first experience pain.

Yes, family matters in the lives and wellbeing of our children. When you notice your child struggling or they share that fact, it never hurts to look in the mirror for a wellbeing check. And that does place responsibility on parents, but our children are our greatest gift, and something that good doesn't come without a price. In parenting, the responsibility begins at a child's birth; even the CDC says, "Children rely on parents to provide them with the care they need to be happy and healthy, and to grow and develop well."

It's humorous that a government agency like the CDC needs to spend time telling us the role of parents. And some parents are no doubt thinking to themselves now that the CDC is aiming that statement at broken families with distracted parents who aren't placing their children front and center on most days. However, almost every parent needs this reminder, about both the role model and the structure and hands-on guidance they are providing. The research is clear about the impact of both.

In a 2022 study, Columbia University's Mailman School of Public Health found that more and more U.S. adolescents are using marijuana and vaping. The researchers pointed to less structured time and more time spent with peers rather than adults, including parents, as reasons for the increased use. In other words, the study validated what has long been assumed: parents who allow their children more room to run free socially with peers dramatically increase the odds that their teens will misuse substances.

"Substance use prevalence decreases across decades were largest for the groups defined by significant paid employment or high levels of social time, either with low engagement in other activities or lower levels of supervision, though these groups had the highest initial prevalence of each variety of substance use," said Noah Kreski, MPH, of the Department of Epidemiology at Columbia's Mailman School.

We learned this the hard way in our family. Like most parents, we considered our family close, and with our first child, William, we had many rules, including limiting nights spent away from home and time hanging out at friends' homes. By the time Hudson, our second child, became a teenager, he had several close friends from church and the neighborhood whom he liked to hang out with outside our home. The environments seemed safe, and we didn't have the same determination we began with, so considerable time outside the home with friends turned into far too much time outside the home with friends. Still, we had no warning signs—until we faced an undeniable one.

Only when Hudson entered substance treatment for nearly dying of an overdose did we begin to learn what transpired. He spent hours in the basement of a friend's house, a basement that had its own entrance and privacy from the rest of the house. The friend's parents were older, with married children, and weren't engaged with the boys, just as we weren't. Experimentation with marijuana in early high school became regular marijuana use in later high school. Periodic drinking became routine bingeing. Three of the four boys who routinely hung out together in the basement in high school are now sober in their early thirties, and two of them went to treatment.

Now, I can look back at the research and understand that statistically if we'd kept Hudson at home more often than not, he might not have struggled so much with substance use. And if he had, we'd have noticed it earlier and had the opportunity to get him to treatment sooner. But the parent's role also involves what happens in the home when children are there. Routinely I get calls from parents who are upset that their child is using marijuana daily, and wondering how and why their child could do such a thing. They don't make the connection to their own daily alcohol consumption, which begins at about 5 PM and ends most evenings in a slight slur before bed.

A parent's influence on their child is profound, especially when the relationship is close or the child looks up to the parent. "Dad's so cool. He makes people laugh, earns good money, and takes us to concerts. I want to be like him."

They're doing like Dad—it's just from a bong, not a bottle.

It sounds harsh, I know, and I'm not casting the first stone. Hardly. I lived this life, and paid a dear price for it. I'll never forget the eye-opening experience of hearing my son Hudson tell a story about me that occurred on a family beach vacation when he was in middle school—long before he began hanging out in the friend's basement daily in high school. Hudson delivered this story as the one he got to share about me during the family day when he was in an intensive outpatient center for treatment. Hudson told how our family was on a trip with my wife's sister and her children—his aunt and first cousins. He explained how we had finished a family dinner, featuring homemade shrimp pasta and multiple bottles of wine for the adults. We were doing the dishes and clearing the table when he and his cousins approached me wanting ice cream money. Their plan was to secure the money and take a walk to get a cone. Feeling like a doting father, I dug out a twenty-dollar bill from my pocket, saying, "Here you go."

My perspective was that this was a scene of me being a good father, engaging with my son. Hudson's perspective, though, was that I, inebriated, folded my wallet and attempted to place it into my right back pocket but missed and tried again before landing it in the slot. He explained how, standing beside me with his cousins, he was embarrassed—for me, himself, and our family. After giving Hudson the money, I poured myself another half glass of wine, finished cleaning the kitchen while laughing and sloshing through a story or two that seemed funny in the moment, and went to bed, unaware of the embarrassment my actions had caused.

It was the Fourth of July week at the beach. We weren't driving or breaking the law. But I broke a moral code as a parent by being an embarrassment to my son because I was too tipsy from wine to get my wallet smoothly back into my pocket.

When I tell this story to parents, some fathers get upset. "What?" they'll say. "You're being too hard on yourself. You are a grown man and do what you want to do."

That's true; it's just that I didn't want to do that. My substance use disorder was doing the talking, representing me to my son. And it might be easier to overlook if the signs weren't so clear that such behavior, occurring more than just that one time, contributed significantly to Hudson's substance use disorder.

The apple doesn't fall far from the tree, as they say.

And experts in generational addiction agree that although an adult alcoholic's issues may have developed slowly over many years, over decades perhaps, their child will frequently get from zero to dead or near dead in their substance use disorder before the parent can even figure out what's going on.

It's like the parent slowly kills themselves while the child does it at the speed of lightning.

There is a plausible reason for this, namely that *things have changed*. While the parent's alcohol abuse may span thirty years before the resulting disaster, the child's substance abuse involving alcohol, 300 to 400 percent stronger marijuana, counterfeit pills, or cocaine laced with fentanyl is a race car looking for an imminent crash.

That's how it was for my sons. We didn't understand this. We didn't understand much of what was happening, and I especially didn't understand how my behavior contributed to their struggles. But I learned that once a child is in recovery, the impact a parent has on them is enormous. When Hudson worked on his sobriety, we forged a supportive bond, thriving off the role model we saw in each other. I'm sure to this day, more than a decade later, that he's got everything to do with my success, and he's quick to credit me with the same.

BE YOUR BEST YOU

Building our resilience, the ability to recover from difficulties and keep moving, is the most significant investment we can make in ourselves. In banking terms, it pays dividends equal to 6 million percent or more. And I'm not talking about your child, here, though resilience will likely be a part of their story in navigating healthily away from substance misuse or battling in recovery if they suffer from addiction. Now, I'm talking about you, the parent (or educator). Today's children and students need us, and you in particular, especially if you, too, struggle with too much time invested in substance misuse. And you deserve joy, too.

If substances have taken your joy, and life's gotten a bit harder and less enjoyable than it should be, it's time to pick yourself up, dust yourself off, and create a toolbox for change so you can be your best and provide your children and students the role model they deserve. It starts with a decision, and it will benefit you—and your family—more than you can imagine. It will likely also change the course of your family for generations, stopping the hand-me-down nature of substance misuse in its tracks and forging a new path toward wellbeing. It takes a first step, powered by resilience and sustained by joy.

We all have something, a battle with food or alcohol, or pain inherited from our parents, to grapple with. For me, it was a bit of all of that, and I wanted to give up, truly, I did. I thought about it more than once. Somehow, I kept going through the hardest times because I believed a better day might come, and then faith and introspection finally helped me get over the line and into recovery. I assessed my life—the people in it, the things in it—and decided I didn't have to spend any time with anyone or anything I didn't want to spend time with. I took control of my life and found the strength to stand up straight, look at myself in the mirror, and trust and respect the reflection.

If you, by chance, are also struggling with drinking too much, or spending too much time with other substances, I hope you will decide this very moment to take back control of your life, for yourself and for your family. "A parent with a SUD [substance use disorder], who is mood altered, preoccupied with getting high or spending significant amounts of time recovering from the effects of substances, may miss the opportunities to foster healthy attachment," wrote the authors of a 2013 journal article, "The Impact of Substance Use Disorders on Families and Children: From Theory to Practice." "Healthy attachment is a psychological immune system of sorts. Just as humans need a physiological immune system to fight off disease and illness, likewise, the relational attachment system provides protection against psychological problems and illness. Without a healthy attachment system, a child is much more vulnerable to stress and therefore more susceptible to having problems with trauma, anxiety, depression, and other mental illness."

Perhaps you are not in a spot as low as I reached, and I hope and pray that is the case. Likely, you are not in a low place at all. It's just that from our foundation, wherever it lies, we can gain strength and find joy we didn't have before. And as we stand taller and stronger, and become more confident, approachable, and empathetic—qualities that come with more emotional strength and depth—we provide energy to the shining lights all around us, our family in particular. I hope you'll trust that in helping your child or children, you must also help yourself. It starts there and comes from a foundation that can always use improvement.

In lean manufacturing, it's called striving for continuous improvement. Just because we can assemble a door on a car in three minutes today doesn't mean we can't learn to do it better. In a former life, when I was writing business and leadership books, I got access to Toyota to study its manufacturing efficiency, which helped the company become one of the world's largest, most profitable, and most reliable automakers. The consistent focus on improvement powered that success, and a backbone of the process was the "rid all that adds no value" principle.

In life, we take on new habits and behaviors, and the unhelpful ones pile up like unneeded belongings in a garage or closet. We don't need them; they clutter our lives, but we keep them anyway. That's how it is for many people with alcohol, for instance. They don't qualify as suffering from substance use disorder, but they also don't see the value any longer. But they continue to drink because someone invites them to a party and serves a drink. It's what you do.

Several years after writing the book on Toyota, I thumbed back through its pages, looking at the lessons of lean manufacturing, and realized that I could apply the best one to my life and benefit. Since then, I've made "rid all that adds no value" a pillar of my foundation, and it's worked. Or if people want time that I'm not comfortable giving, or if how I would spend the time doesn't fit my mission, I'll decline, politely. If my carbohydrate consumption has gone too far (a challenge I face in not drinking alcohol is using food to replace it), I'll back off. And, yes, I stopped drinking alcohol due to the "rid all that adds no value" principle.

I stopped to save my family, myself, and my career. What I didn't understand, though, was how much time, focus, and energy alcohol wasted in my life even when I wasn't drinking too much. Just a couple of glasses of wine left me a tad foggy and less productive the next day, but I'd become so used to the feeling that I thought it was normal. Once I stopped drinking, I saved my family, myself, and my career, and the further I went on the journey, the more rewards added up. Friends who've quit have asked me, "Why didn't you tell me I'd end up with so much more [money, happiness, time]?"

"You wouldn't have understood," I'd explain.

But I can't sit silent any longer. Life is a pendulum, and we live in a world of excess that makes it so easy for the pendulum to swing too far away from joy. We start chasing things that provide immediate gratification, and it's hard to stop pursuing fleeting moments of happiness. The biggest payoff, though, is less influence from things and more nourishment for the soul.

It's why even after experiencing the most joyful, rewarding decade of my life, beyond anything I previously imagir

I still seek counseling because I want to grow and gain more self-awareness. It's like running, or going to the gym. With more distance run or weight lifted, you gain the strength to do more. Soon you can run or lift like you couldn't imagine. Our emotional development works the same way. We can regress or move forward, but it's rarely stagnant.

I choose forward. I hope you choose forward, too.

That's why when my wife, Kent, suggested I add counseling to my routine one year ago, I didn't say no. Admittedly, my immediate response was "I'm happier than I've ever been." Within minutes, however, I knew she was right. Great can always be greater, and we don't want to take our joy for granted.

Thus, I put my ego and stubbornness aside and began counseling, and by the second visit I was thanking my wife and pinpointing two tangible, positive changes that made my life better. Even therapists see therapists for tune-ups.

It's not that something is wrong with us. Our strengths are weaknesses and vice versa, so we humans are within a brushstroke of having or causing frustration at any given moment. I've also learned, through experience, the value children gain from having strong, emotionally healthy parents. The more emotional IQ you display, making sense and peace with the world and others, the more your children will have.

It's about them, but so much of it is also about you, particularly when it comes to mental health and substance use disorder. Your mental health matters as much as your child's if they are struggling, because your light can lead the way. And you matter, and your entire family matters. So, wherever you are, I hope you'll take this nudge to cultivate your resilience, take a ride away from the frustration and darkness, and embark on a rich and rewarding journey of growth and wellbeing.

TAKEAWAYS

- Substance use disorder is a family issue because the entire family unit is affected.
- Parents are primary role models for children and can set a healthy model within a family.
- Students who spend more social time with friends, away from adults, are more likely to use substances like marijuana.
- Resilience pays healthy dividends to all members of the family.

10

DEVELOP A TOOLBOX

I frequently get to meet and engage with many high school and college students who are thriving and happy—they are joyful. When I look at the characteristics these thriving students possess, common themes emerge. It's no coincidence that they match up almost perfectly with characteristics identified in Gallup surveys and multiple other studies as factors that contribute to human joy and wellbeing.

When I first began speaking to students in schools, I didn't put a list of suggested tips on a slide because this seemed too simple, insulting almost. I'm going to tell a college student it's important to walk or exercise regularly, and sleep more? Right. They'll never listen.

Wrong.

I tried it, introducing the "Student Toolbox" in a presentation slide, and the audience looked intently, then one, and another, and another stood up and took a photo of the image. "Everyone needs a toolbox," I said. A student near the front raised a hand. "What's a toolbox?" he asked.

"A toolbox," I explained, "is where you store the things you need to keep your life of joy intact. It's always at hand; you know and understand the tools in the box, and can utilize them with confidence and comfort, greatly increasing your odds for joy." Here are my student tips, with a detailed explanation of each.

THE STUDENT TOOLBOX

- Each day – substance = WIN
- Value sleep like the air you breathe.
- Live in the moment; embrace the calm.
- Activity (like walking or running) sends invigorating blood to the brain and body.
- Remember, you are not alone; mental health challenges are common.
- Ask for help: getting counseling earlier and more often makes a difference.
- Protect your toolbox at all costs.
- Identify the drug dealer (invest in healthy relationships).
- Earn what you get and/or find ways to serve.
- Be intentional about social media (own it, so it doesn't own you).
- Believe in something greater than yourself (have faith).

Each Day – Substance = WIN

A student approached me after a talk with an air of failure. I'd explained how delayed or less substance use for teenagers greatly increases odds of a lifetime of joy by reducing substance use disorder risks. He'd used alcohol and marijuana a few times in the ninth grade and assumed there was no going back, as if once he'd crossed the line and experimented, he'd subscribed to a lifetime of use.

"Did you like it?"

"No," he said. "The marijuana made me feel scared, strange. The alcohol made me feel out of control. I didn't like either that much, but I did try them again."

He dropped his head.

"Okay," I said, "look at me. You are not a failure, and not even close. Here you are, reaching out, thinking about it. That's good!"

He looked up.

"Here's the deal," I continued. "Less use is more. Every day you let your brain develop as nature intended, mature without interference from powerful substances, is another day of investment in yourself, in your future. What you did is done, and it's in the past. Each day is a new opportunity to invest in yourself."

He smiled, extended his hand, and delivered a firm handshake.

"Yes, sir," he said. "I understand."

That was three years ago. I don't know how that young man is doing, but I know that his outlook changed on that day. He felt ashamed that he'd used alcohol and marijuana, but then felt freed once he learned that the present moment and the future were in his hands. Nothing was lost.

We must remind students that every day without substance misuse is an investment in themselves, regardless of the past.

Value Sleep Like the Air You Breathe

I've been approached by hundreds of struggling students in recent years who face myriad issues on the mental health spectrum as well as some level of substance misuse. I give the same advice to them all: "Get counseling, and some rest now— you look like you could use it." Because they do; each of them looks so tired.

I've yet to have a struggling student approach me who doesn't look like they've missed eight sleeps in a row or more, or like they've slept on a bed of rocks. Even if they are engaged while talking, they are choking off yawns. They're so exhausted that I wonder what would happen if they just went to bed for redeeming rest. Maybe they would wake up refreshed and see clearly what they should already know, and they wouldn't need me to tell them, "Get to counseling and get some rest now."

Live in the Moment; Embrace the Calm

There's a difference between loneliness and being alone. Loneliness can occur even when we're surrounded by people. Time spent being alone is our time to shine as humans, moments when our creativity and ideation can and will flow, if we learn to let it.

Being alone takes practice, and most young people aren't good at it. They'll avoid it at all costs. That's because they don't know how to spend time alone, in the quiet. Trying to sit at home quietly is more challenging in a world driven by social media, after all, when friends doing something have you at their fingertips for show-and-tell. *We're at the lake. We're at the ice cream shop. We're pregaming before the game.* However, time spent alone in the quiet and calm forms the bedrock of our foundation as humans. It's when we carve emotional depth, learn to manage our thoughts and feelings, and craft inner strength that yields high self-esteem. It's when our creative fountain runs deepest. It's when we learn that we are strong and can survive and thrive on our own.

Activity (Like Walking or Running) Sends Invigorating Blood to the Brain and Body

We use substances to change how we feel. Many students wouldn't imagine walking into a party without pregaming with a substance, just as many adults go in extra hard after a long, hard week for those Friday night cocktails. Users want a mental shift, so they take in substances to alter the brain, the three-pound mass of organ that controls our life. Substances hit the brain with a pleasurable reward in much the same way that natural behaviors like eating, sex, or social stimulation do. It's just that substances are so much more powerful than these milder experiences. Consider how the brain gets a pleasure punch from engaging with friends versus snorting cocaine. We were designed to follow the milder, natural responses but chase after the power-punch response that a strong drug like cocaine delivers.

It's easy to imagine how the brain reacts to such bursts of pleasure—it wants more. That's why once we start giving our most cherished organ artificial stimulation with drugs, it can be hard to turn back.

It's better, I explain to students, to give our brains frequent natural stimulation than to feed it something unsustainable, like cocaine or opiates. Take the classic walk, as an example. Most of us who've learned and love the art of walking know any walk is good. Runners say the same about their experiences. The reason is simple: When we move, blood circulation increases, taking oxygen and natural nourishment to the brain and throughout our body. We instantly become more alive and alert, and our mood improves. It's why when I'm working on a project requiring creativity, I'll take periodic breaks and hit the streets, walking. Without fail, the ideas flow. Most of my decent ideas have come to me on a walk.

Too many young people don't take advantage of these natural micro highs, the benefit of using activity to enhance how we feel. College students tell me they were so busy in high school, playing sports and doing other activities, that they quickly lost interest in physical activity, once it wasn't a necessary part of being on a team. So they get stagnant; they lose the natural stimulation that once helped sustain them, which makes unnatural stimulation more appealing. Thus, I try to reinforce to college students the importance of activity, including regular walks, running, or games like pickup basketball or soccer. It's a simple act, but such actions can make all the difference toward making a day a good day, providing natural weaponry against anxiety and depression with additional healthy benefits.

Remember, You Are Not Alone; Mental Health Challenges Are Common

You'd think that by nearly a quarter of the way into the twenty-first century we wouldn't have to explain to our population that almost everyone encounters a mental health issue at some point in their life, and that for many of us it will be a significant challenge. And it's not that this messaging is not out there, because it is. It's just that when a person is trapped while suffering, they can feel so alone, and the fear of stigma can paralyze them. A 2016–2017 University of Michigan survey revealed that nearly 50 percent of students polled agreed with the statement "Most people would think less of someone who has received mental health treatment."

In my experience helping students get to counseling or treatment, I see this play out weekly, with most who agree to get help providing an initial caveat—they don't want anyone to know or to see them walk into a building or office for assistance. I'm convinced, therefore, that teens and college students need constant reminders, namely peer-to-peer education and support, that help break the stigma, letting them know that mental health issues are common and they are not alone. Parents and educators can play a crucial role in this reinforcement, with conversations that humanize and even celebrate humans who struggle and get help.

Ask for Help: Getting Counseling Earlier and More Often Makes a Difference

Once the wall of stigma comes down and students are willing to engage in counseling or treatment, the natural tendency for many is to agree to go, but to try to bargain their way out of it later, putting it off. The unknown is scary and feels uncomfortable, of course. The results for students who go earlier and regularly are undeniable, however, and recovery is attainable to almost everyone since most universities and communities have resources for those who don't have insurance or can't otherwise afford it. It's true that since the COVID-19 pandemic and the ensuing mental health epidemic, many counselors are booked and getting an appointment isn't always easy. A few phone calls and persistence, though, typically land an appointment. And I tell students that if they call for an appointment and are told the calendar is full, they should ask for recommendations for other counselors or groups in the area that might be accepting appointments.

It's also good advice for students and parents to locate

counseling options when arriving on a college campus. Each year, I get calls when freshmen arrive on campus, asking about resources.

One young woman was excited about the start of the next stage of her life in college but fearful that recent panic attacks might get out of hand and she'd have nowhere to turn. Kelly explained that her mother suffers from alcohol use disorder but has been successful in recovery for over twenty-five years, so she's learned through osmosis and her mother's sharing about tools for managing her feelings. She had avoided consuming alcohol with any frequency until her senior year of high school, when two or three times a month she and her friends turned up the energy on their drinking as a "rite of passage" tied to their upcoming graduation. Kelly noticed that her panic attacks flared more frequently when she was drinking but couldn't pinpoint a direct association. "It was a coincidence, perhaps," she said. Kelly knew, however, that more drinking was likely in store for her first year—she planned to rush and pledge a sorority—and feared panic attacks might flare in step with that increased alcohol use.

"I'm excited about college but afraid I'll be alone when a panic attack strikes, unsure of what to do," Kelly said.

"My advice to incoming freshmen is to identify a counseling center and counselor upon arrival the same way they would make note of the restaurants they might frequent on campus and in town."

"Go ahead and get a local counselor?" she asked.

"That's your call. If you feel you need a local one now, then yes, now. If you feel more comfortable just identifying one in case you need them, great. But since you have panic attacks, also make a list to keep at hand of the student health center and local emergency centers. The more knowledge you have of resources, the more comfort you'll have when you need it most."

Protect Your Toolbox at All Costs

I tell students eager to fight for their wellbeing to take the toolbox seriously, list the tools they want to focus on maintaining, and keep them close. Others, friends in particular, will try to interrupt their dedication to the list of tools, because their friends' wants and needs will revolve around themselves. I tell students, "Say you need more sleep on a night your friends are determined to go out, perhaps to celebrate a birthday or to meet someone. They may try to persuade you until you break down and join them, because they're unconcerned that protecting your sleep is a key item on your list. It's about them, not you."

Substance use persuasion is much the same.

"Let's do shots!"

"I don't want to."

"Come on! Loosen up."

"I wanted to be home by midnight."

"Here, I've poured us shots. On three."

Again, I tell students, "It's about them, not you."

Family members, too, want students' time and attention. I've seen many college students, for example, struggle to keep up with family messages on their phone throughout the day. Friends are constantly pinging them and they've got classwork and club meetings, but all day long their mother, sister, and father light up their phone with texts.

"How was class?"

"What will you do for dinner?"

"Your brother has a basketball game tonight. Call us and we'll tell you how he did."

"How's your day? Are you happy?"

This type of communication is an endless distraction, making the students homesick and unable to manage the barrage of messages. Family support is vital for students, even for college students. Still, there's a point where it becomes more than they can handle in a day, and three family members sending messages from morning to night is typically beyond that point.

For students, it's about maintaining that support but establishing through honest dialogue with loved ones what's hurting more than helping. They don't want loneliness, not at all. But even if they want constant attention daily, it's more than they can emotionally manage in a day.

Identify the Drug Dealer
(Invest in Healthy Relationships)

When most people hear the words "drug dealer," they get an image of a shadowy figure, working from a street corner or a dark house, peddling illegal substances. But the drug dealer is not who you think it is, particularly among high school and college students.

The drug dealer is typically someone your student knows, perhaps their best friend, teammate, fraternity member, or roommate. I know this because my son William, the honors college student and track athlete at a SEC school, first introduced my son Hudson, his younger brother, to some dangerous substances, including Xanax. When Hudson was found nearly dead at the fraternity house from an accidental overdose, the Xanax had mixed with alcohol and made him pass out and choke on his vomit. William stood by pale and sickened in the emergency room watching the doctor pound on Hudson's chest, trying to get his heart beating. William told us later he'd made a deal with God in that moment—spare Hudson's life and he'd quit doing drugs.

Hudson came back to life and answered his prayer. And William tried, yes, he did, to stop doing drugs. William found sobriety for months before relapsing and dying of an accidental overdose. In those months of his recovery, we talked, and he shared how substance use disorder makes people lose their mind in some respects. You'll do things that don't make sense, like introducing your younger brother, whom you love like nobody else on this earth, to a deadly drug like Xanax.

"Here," William said, "try these. They're amazing."

I share that story with students and fraternity members frequently since my sons William and Hudson were brothers, but also "brothers" in a fraternity, the same fraternity I belonged to. William loved his brother so much, yet he introduced him to Xanax and other drugs and kept them coming, I'll explain, before asking, "What does that make William, to my son Hudson?"

Eyes get watery. A few squirm in their seats.

"Yes, let me just say it. William, in that instance, was Hudson's drug dealer.

"It hurts me to say that, it really does. I loved William so much, and miss him every day. And I'm just sick about that fact, but it goes hand in hand with substance use disorder. It's not uncommon behavior, and we'll do the worst things, like giving dangerous drugs to our brother."

I tell them about William arriving from college and making close friends with a member of his pledge class from Atlanta.

They didn't have too much in common besides the fraternity and the fact that both had well-hidden and well-developed substance use disorder. Soon, the friend used his big-city connections to introduce William to new substances, keeping them in ready supply.

"What did that make William's friend? You got it. William's friend was his drug dealer."

I knew the friend's family, and they were the finest people. Their son, like my William, was among the finest as well. But they struggled with the disease. I'm sure that this type of inexplicable behavior inspired the phrase "the devil made them do it."

Before you judge my William, or his roommate, take note that almost every high school and college student I know who has used or uses illegal drugs, ranging from marijuana and cocaine to MDMA (Molly) to counterfeit Adderall, gets it from someone they know. It comes from a brother, team member, or classmate. Sure, there's the community middle person taking delivery from the distributors. But it's usually a case of students involving students, making introductions, and helping with deliveries.

I wish it wasn't so. But it is. And most of those involved students are not stupid and reckless so much as they are sick, suffering from a disease that tells them both that it's normal to peddle these substances and that they need the money from their efforts to get more drugs for themselves. It's just how it goes, heartbreakingly so. They don't have their buyers' interests at heart; they are driven by their disease. That's why I tell every young person I can that the company they keep has so much to do with the joy they receive.

The drug dealers are not who you think they are. That's

why the company we keep has so much to do with the roads we travel. I tell students to respect all people but only invest in healthy relationships—with those who have their best interests at heart.

Earn What You Get and/or Find Ways to Serve

Self-esteem determines so much of our mental health and behavior. When it's low, we slump, and when it's high, we thrive. It's a matter of understanding how we can elevate our self-esteem as a high-yield personal investment. For most humans of all ages, self-sufficiency is a building block of self-esteem. That doesn't mean young people must be thrown into providing everything for themselves when resources are available. Not at all. But there's a consistent story told on college campuses: students who work summers or part-time during semesters or serve as a volunteer in student or community organizations are more engaged and joyful.

When students or parents ask me for advice, I deliver this with conviction because the dividends I see among students as early as middle school are so high. The issue in this world where the haves have so much is that we parents want our children to have everything we didn't. It's not that we desire to spoil them; it's just that we want them to have everything we feel they deserve.

That's how we were with William, our firstborn. Because he made good grades, became fluent in Spanish, was all-state in track and field, and participated in church youth group, we tried to give him so much. William got a new car when he turned sixteen, he spent a summer in Spain after his junior year in high school, he went skiing with friends at Christmas, and he always had enough money in his wallet.

But William was broke in self-esteem.

And we buried him at twenty-three.

At that moment, we sat our other two children, Hudson and Mary Halley, down for a talk. They were both still in college, Hudson a junior and Mary Halley a freshman. We explained that our job as parents wasn't to give them more things; our job was to give them more love.

"We've got to do better," I said. "We tried to make sure William had everything, but we're going to do this differently. I hope you'll thank us one day and forgive us on this day, but you'll have to contribute substantially from this day on to your college and living and social expenses. We're still contributing. It's just that now you're in with us significantly."

They were in mourning as we were for losing William, and they might have complained if not for the lingering shock of his passing. While it didn't seem fair that they'd get less because William had struggled, they also said they understood why.

"We can't take the risk of losing another," I said.

Hudson got a job making pizzas, and months later he was selling craft popsicles to downtown tourists from a pushcart. Mary Halley became a professional babysitter. They contributed toward their college tuition, books, gas, and apartments. We invited them over for dinners several times a week and took them to movies. We laughed more, despite our family tragedy, and loved more.

Their grades soared, as did their self-esteem, despite the struggles they faced (Hudson was new in sobriety after his near-death experience, and Mary Halley was in counseling for her eating disorder). Within months, they thanked us, saying they understood and appreciated our contribution more because they better understood its value. They enjoyed contributing to their future and direction, which played a crucial role in their recovery.

Most importantly, it allowed my wife and me to focus more on providing our remaining two children the riches of love and attention. And that's what they needed most.

Be Intentional About Social Media
(Own It, So It Doesn't Own You)

This is the advice I give to students about social media: just because it's there, just because it feels like it's where everyone else is, doesn't mean you must be on social media every hour on the hour, day after day, peering into others' airbrushed lives. There are benefits to social media. You can announce life changes to the world on your terms or write a caption expressing the feelings of the season. But when your log-in becomes a continual scroll, which steals valuable time and shifts your feelings toward where you are not or what you don't have, it's time to log off and do something else. Consider whether your stress level increases after long periods of time scrolling through social media, and whether it contributes to procrastination and ensuing guilt. Or if it provokes feelings of inferiority and nervousness. Any or all of these suggest change is needed.

If notifications are your thing, turn them off. If doomscrolling is your thing and wasting that time brings guilt, delete the app from your phone.

It's not necessary or reasonable to see every post or post your every move, and nobody needs too much of you either. You are just seeking instant feedback from incessant stories and posts, the same type of activity that's bothersome when you see others doing it. Leave that pastime behind; it's among your least productive activities of any day. Set boundaries and rules, and if you find you can't adhere to them, then face a reality: you've become addicted, it's negatively affecting your life, and more drastic removal steps might be required.

The key is owning it, so it doesn't own you. Develop a plan for using it by asking yourself: What do I want from social media?

Most of us want a presence in, a window to, and a megaphone for the world for when those things are needed. And that's the key—needed. Start with that baseline and determine the daily and weekly time investment necessary to meet your objective of using social media for enjoyable and beneficial purposes. The freedom you will find in regaining hours sans distraction can give a boost to joy and help set you on your desired path.

Believe in Something Greater than Yourself (Have Faith)

The things we covet and chase, believing they'll bring us happiness and joy, are mostly a waste of time. A little money helps, but not a lot—the more we have, the more we want. Those lottery tickets? A waste of money, because a win will most assuredly damage your life and generations of your family. Joy is not the happy hour with friends, or the new car—those are fleeting. It's faith or religion—believing in something bigger than yourself, like God—that provides a deep sense of meaning, purpose, and contented joy.

Half of this book could focus on this aspect of wellbeing

because study after study shows we are most grounded and at peace with ourselves when we have faith. I'm not here to tell you exactly what that looks like for you and your children because it's different for everyone, including Christians, even members of the same church.

Faith changed my life and has everything to do with my recovery. I had taught a young adult Sunday school class for years and considered myself a Christian, but looking back, I didn't have faith at all. I didn't sincerely, truly believe that I'm just a speck on this earth and there must be a higher power than me. On a trip with my son William, driving across the country in a historic snowstorm, I first recognized that I was powerless—I was feeling grief and angst trying to manage a world I couldn't lasso. I've had peace and joy from that moment forth. It hasn't always been easy. My faith was challenged the day I found William dead, the day Hudson nearly died, and the day I learned I had an unusual and risky cancer. But faith guided me through those moments, and the joy never left.

It's not that we won't cry with faith and feel sadness. Indeed, grief and sadness are so much a part of living and faith that experiencing them is critical to finding and keeping joy. We try so hard to numb our feelings, to avoid feeling sad, but, in fact, embracing appropriate sadness, and learning to manage and even embrace the emotion, is a path to joy. We can't have one without the other, and faith can provide the strength and comfort to guide us in periods of difficultly (professional help is always recommended for mental health issues; we're talking everyday challenges of life and loneliness).

I'm hardly the evangelist. Spirituality is deeply personal,

and different for everyone, as I've said. What it does and means for me is mine, and what it does and means for you is yours. For instance, a man in New York approached me after hearing my wife and me talk at a meeting, where we'd mentioned that faith and believing in something bigger than oneself is a key to joy and a life without substances. Yes, there's a reason Alcoholics Anonymous has "find your highest power" as a cornerstone of its healing journey. For me, that is God. As the man in New York said, it might be yoga for someone else.

"We go to the church of yoga weekly," he said.

I smiled.

"It's not really a church," he said. "But we go to yoga and bring a spirituality to it about the people in our lives, the environment, and all the healing that can be done."

I saw his peace and the comfort he found in what he believed.

There's a reason a majority of Americans consider themselves Christian.

There's also a reason that American Christianity is in rapid decline—we're taking the joy from it by conflating faith with politics beyond reason. Non-Christian politicians use faith as a weapon to scare Christians into supporting them. Christian politicians use faith as a weapon to denigrate humans, God's children, who disagree with them.

So I'm not saying that the political type of faith can help students, or any of us, find and keep joy. I'm saying that believing in something holy, caring, and bigger than us all can give students the hope and comfort they need to keep marching onward.

More than anything else in this book, the research on this lesson is undeniable: faith, or belief in something bigger than ourselves, increases the odds for joy.

For students, it's challenging, however. On their own for the first time, many aren't leaping from bed on Sunday morning to get to church. It's not for lack of options. Most college campuses and communities have dozens of options, including student groups sponsored by churches and student-focused ministries within churches. I live in the heart of the Bible Belt, and the ratio of faith leaders focused on ministry to students is tremendous. Still, faith often isn't the first thing on the mind of students when they get to college. Those who become involved, however, receive a tangible benefit in terms of engaged relationships with adults, who provide caring and identifiable support aligned with the students' best interests, which also contributes to their joy and wellbeing.

Then there's the "something bigger than oneself" element. Faith is an easy path for believers because there are built-in, readily available networks and programming. Many students, though, will chase their passions and create their own "bigger than themselves" path, dedicated to breaking the stigma around addiction and mental health, solving world hunger, or advocating for LGBTQ rights. Such work delivers tangible benefits, making a better world while simultaneously giving the individual doing the work a gratifying, foundational reward from aspiration and work shared with others—the sense of belonging.

Our son Hudson is an excellent example of how faith can save a soul. As a freshman and sophomore, he was driven by the substance use disorder that owned him, spending more time focused on girls, friends, music, and substances, although he'd been consistently involved in a Christian high school small group led by an associate pastor for four years before college. After his near death from accidental overdose, Hudson refortified himself with faith, moving in with friends of faith and getting involved with a church and its associated ministry. He also fell in love with the church of the outdoors, God's most incredible creation, and that brought a spiritual element as he fly-fished, rock climbed, and hiked his way to lasting sobriety. Hudson benefited directly from his belief in something bigger and his engagement with friends, church members, and the enriching outdoors.

DOES THE TOOLBOX WORK?

Yes, indeed, the toolbox works. Many of these principles and tactics are deployed along with others by people who have had long-term success in recovery, validating the impact of these tools. Also, there's considerable research about how faith, quality sleep, exercise, and other practices on the list help us achieve health and wellbeing.

Your child's toolbox should be personalized, though. What works well for one person might work best for another with tweaks or adjustments. Helping your child develop a toolbox is about starting a conversation with them to let them know they control their destiny. Having a plan to find and keep joy and wellbeing pays off. It's much more difficult for any of us to wake up and find ourselves at the mercy of others who don't hold our best interests. They may care about us, sure. But whatever they deal with can't help but affect what they want from us.

Your child's joy and wellbeing require a plan; they need to take control of what they want by developing their toolbox. It's a collection of strategies that when implemented in whole or in part on an ongoing basis leads to a richer, more fulfilling life.

TAKEAWAYS

- Getting the best results in life usually requires a plan. Students with a personalized toolbox can find more joy.
- Developing brains need consistent rest and activity.
- Healthy relationships make a difference.
- Believing in something bigger than oneself can give purpose and joy.

11

THE ROAD TO WELLBEING

I t's a bit overwhelming, what students face, I know. I wish I could deliver a different scenario than the one I've described, but *things have changed* so fast that students are at high risk and need help navigating. If the challenge was just smartphones and social media, or the romanticized alcohol culture, or just the more potent marijuana and counterfeit pills, it would be more manageable. It's all of that combined and more, however.

That's why I've delivered here a picture of reality, explaining the serious and daunting challenge students today face. It's because I want your child, and everyone's children, to avoid the common pitfalls. I'm optimistic we can help students one by one to collectively end this mental health and substance misuse crisis. That's because I believe in our youth as well as in parents and educators. It's vital that we face the situation honestly, with open dialogue and a commitment to getting students on the road to wellbeing and recovery. It's not a comfortable conversation, even for me, and I speak or write about it almost every day of the year. I wish we didn't have to talk about it, but we do because these issues are manageable. That's why I focus in on the problems, attempting to identify what's wrong and why. It's not to scare you; that's not my style. It's so you are prepared to help and lead your children.

I've covered a lot of ground in the preceding chapters. The exact best approach to take with each child and their unique challenges will differ, but parents and educators are best prepared when they understand those challenges and their potential solutions. Things have changed so much—from increased technology use and mental health issues to more potent and harmful street marijuana to counterfeit pills and fentanyl—that our children today need our help. The one thing we know that works with almost every teen and college student is improved communication that meets them where they are. We know from experience and it's backed by research: students are less responsive when we preach to them rather than see and hear them. That's why there's no better starting point for your child's journey to wellbeing than improving communication, and that starts with less telling them what they should do or how they should feel and more asking them what they think and how they feel.

ASK OPEN-ENDED QUESTIONS

Before our children reach puberty, we beg them to declare who and what they want to be. We'll say it doesn't matter, but we're asking, prodding, and shepherding, all the while.

What sport or activity will they do? What friends will they have? What camps will they attend? What college will they go to? Will they be valedictorian, or just salutatorian with an emphasis on being social? Will they become a doctor? An engineer? We start this drill the moment we choose their first clothing. We work in the directions we want, providing tutoring, year-round coaching outside team practice, and social support, including phone, money, car, and clothes if we can afford them, and even if not.

We've become excellent at child shaping—wanting our offspring to have so much more of what we deem to be good that we lead them with loaded questions down the trails of our desires. Nearly half the college students I meet have a parent in tow, as if they're signed up for the experience, too, helping their child make their class selections, talking to them for hours each day, inquiring about when they eat and where. But the desire for them to have such a "perfect" college experience can ensure the opposite because true joy is elusive without learning, failing, and feeling on their own terms.

Most of us achieve nothing without the struggle that precedes. Our failure fuels success, and our heartache can lead us to love.

We are wired with a range of emotions. Debilitating sadness requires professional help, but the sadness we get from moments of mistake or aloneness is natural—healthy, even. Humans can't experience joy without sadness; it's a necessary balance. It's just that most parents don't want their children to suffer even a moment of failure or despair, so they'll follow them to college to do it all, even if it promises to rob their children of true joy down the road.

I'm not judging parents for this impulse. I've done it, and I remember too well reading through the journal my late son William kept in treatment and seeing his comment that "my dad made most of my decisions for me."

Ouch.

In my mind, I was helping steer my son to success. In his mind, he followed me, thinking I was right. But I wasn't.

If I could talk directly to William today, I wouldn't ask what kind of angel he wants to be at age thirty-five. I wouldn't ask who the angels are he wants to be like. I'd ask, "*How* does it feel to be an angel watching me stumble over myself?" Or I'd ask, "*How* did it feel when you kept taking drugs but wanted to quit?" And I'd listen deeply to his response, soaking up every word to better understand my son.

What if you shifted the equation with your child, worrying not about what they can become or who they will do it with but *how* they feel? Not who or what, but *how*.

There's considerable upside to asking children open-ended questions—the most substantial benefit is you will learn what you didn't know about your child. If your favorite teddy could talk, what might he say to you? If you could tell your friend group one message they promised to hear, what would it be? Questions that elicit yes-and-no or one-word answers won't suffice. Instead of asking "Do you want to become a doctor or a lawyer?" try "How does it feel when you work a math equation?"

When I talked with a fifth-year accounting student who was poised to take a job at a big Dallas firm but was struggling with depression and marijuana misuse, he listed to me all the reasons he wasn't happy, most of them hard to buy. The addict is good at making contextual excuses and disregarding actuality. He said things like "My parents are in my business," "My girlfriend has been too busy," and "Most of my friends graduated last spring."

"How does doing accounting make you feel?" I asked.

He was stunned at my question, shifting in his chair. For nearly a minute, he couldn't answer.

"Like I need to get up and move," he said.

"Got it," I said. "I guess the marijuana helps you sit there."

He smiled. It was the first smile I'd seen him deliver.

"I've got a lot to think about."

Open-ended questions open your child's mind, and yours, as their responses can inform and surprise and delight deeply. Such questions are also a child's gateway to self-discovery, and if you begin such probing conversations when they are young, the parent-child relationship grows deeper.

Focusing on how today's generation feels rather than thrusting our angst and fears upon them is a starting point for their wellbeing, individually and collectively, since studies show they need to be seen and heard to become whole.

It's a critical starting point. And if you've arrived at this point in the book and decided you want to help your child find and keep the joy they deserve, let me say that seeing and hearing applies to every challenge they may face. Otherwise, imagine your child as a closed lock. You can't open it without the key, and that key is ensuring your child is seen and heard. Example: As you recall from the chapter about smartphones, less is more, and simply approaching your child with rules and tough dialogue about limiting smartphone use won't get the desired result. It may do the opposite. No, they don't have to like it, but engaged discussion and buy-in to get to a healthier relationship with their devices gets the best results.

Once you establish and understand that engagement with your child is of utmost importance, digging in for change gets much more manageable, for a child who's seen and heard is a pussycat, whereas one pushed into a closed corner might bite.

The next step is thinking strategically about change as a whole rather than just picking up one aspect to obsess over, such as "no more than one hour a day of phone time." For a holistic balance, many types of experience are required, though this is easier to achieve than you might think, since one type of experience often feeds into the other. Less smartphone time and more family time yield more engagement and likely more physical activity, for instance.

If you are reading this book, chances are good that someone in your family is struggling in some way. This can feel hard, almost impossible, since other remedies haven't worked. When one suffers from mental health distress, anxiety, depression, an eating disorder, or a substance use disorder, it feels like getting to the other side, where joy and wellbeing reside, is impossible. I've been there, and now, on the other side, I know it was always at my fingertips, just a reach away. Most of us on this journey explain it the same way: *It was like swimming two inches underwater, unaware that so much oxygen was available within the slightest head lift.*

WELLBEING TIPS

- Begin engaged conversations to assess the situation.
- If your child is in emotional distress, has an active eating disorder, or is self-medicating with substances routinely, do not delay counseling and needed support. Now is the moment to act.
- Consider other affected family members who may need counseling or support.
- Develop a wellbeing plan for yourself—remember, your role modeling has a significant impact and can lead the way.

The strategies outlined in this book, supported by engaging young people with open-ended questions and honest conversations that make them feel seen and heard, can help some avoid mental health and substance misuse issues, no doubt. There's plenty of data supporting the benefits of counseling, role-model parents, rest, and exercise. Those suffering can find a path to wellbeing, and they need to know those solutions exist and that you are there to support them in finding the one that's right for them.

"This is all I have to do to find joy?" a student once asked after I showed the toolbox slide.

"Well, there's no guarantee, but I can guarantee that your life will improve if you do these things. Think about it: Get more rest, more time to think, some counseling for introspection, more time with friends who care—all proven to improve mental health—how can you go wrong? It's about investing in yourself. Do these things, and you'll get riches of joy and wellbeing in return.

"Right on," he said.

Indeed, strategies including less time on a smartphone, more sleep, better parental engagement, more physical activity, more time with friends who have their companions' best interests at heart, and waiting to drink alcohol and use marijuana until brains are fully developed will yield healthier teens. It's undeniable. And suppose parents apply some of these commonsense practices to their own lives, swinging the pendulum back toward their own wellbeing. In that case, they'll also experience more peace and joy while simultaneously leading other family members. It's hard to understand why, when we know conclusively that these tools, habits, and processes work, we let our children's lives and ours run in opposite directions. But that's what we do, chasing so-called accomplishments we believe will bring joy when facts reveal another path.

That's why we're in this crisis, with so many students facing angst and substance misuse beginning in middle school and continuing through college. Many parents are so eager not to disrupt the flow and not to get them off track with peers, even if that means missing just one social event, that the long game of building a robust mental health foundation is sacrificed. I was once talking to a parent who was worried their child was anxious but was unwilling to interrupt their child's tilt-a-whirl life. I asked them to see their child as a tree seedling planted in a drought.

"You planted that tree to watch it grow, right?" I asked.

"Sure."

"We're in a drought. Studies show a seedling needs water, or it can't establish roots at its most critical time. Years later, once established and mature, that tree will be able to withstand some drought. But now, what does it need?"

"Water."

"Yes, lots of water. But you are fine dehydrating your child?"

"Well, no, not when you put it that way."

"That's what's happening. Your child needs water, and not just a lot all at once, but on a recurring basis, as part of a healthy, growing lifestyle."

PARENTAL RESPONSIBILITY

You alone can't heal or even save your child, but it's time we accept that holistic care and learning, provided by parents and educators in homes and in classrooms, is as essential as the air children breathe and the food they eat. And because family is the root of our socialization, the effort starts at home.

We readily accept feeding a newborn as our responsibility. Helping our children develop emotionally at the most critical period of their lives so they can thrive throughout a lifetime is perhaps just as important.

The truth is, we don't owe our children the smartphones they want, the social lives they think they deserve. We owe them love. We owe them counseling if they need it, and we owe them boundaries when they need them. We must give them less in things, and more in love, and that love begins with healthy conversations in which they are intricately involved. They learn, and learn well, when we meet them in dialogue where they are, and when they are seen and heard.

The honest, engaged dialogue must begin before middle school and deepen in subject matter throughout puberty, when nature begins to pull children from us. Learn how your children feel, instead of telling them how you want them to feel. Learn who they are and what they want. One thing I know: almost every student, from middle school to college, wants joy, but we must let them speak that truth, so we can help them find that path.

We aren't wired for angst and despair, so this epidemic is unnatural. It's just that the pain has escalated for today's students, and when the pain increases, they'll reach for relief anywhere they can find it—they'll look for affirmation in the wrong relationships or seek a numbing high from counterfeit pills even if they've been warned they likely contain addictive and deadly fentanyl.

But they want joy. The desperately want joy. They've told me over and over again. It's the one common desire shared by almost every young person. And here's the most promising news: we know how to help them get there.

Yes, *things have changed*, but the loving care in the student ecosystem that begins with parents and includes educators has not changed. It's there for students, as passionately as ever. They cannot manage without thoughtful care, listening, and guidance. Remember, it's not so much *what* they are but *how* they are. And you can help them find all the joy they want and deserve.

TAKEAWAYS

- The challenges students face today are daunting, but solutions are at hand. Don't be overwhelmed.
- Open-ended questions are a gateway to engagement.
- Parents should give providing holistic education the same priority as putting food on the table.

Author's Note

We've been busy the last two years building the William Magee Institute for Student Wellbeing at the University of Mississippi, dedicated to saving and changing lives through education, research, and storytelling for students, parents, and educators. It's named after my late son, and the work we do is critical to helping stop this mental health and substance misuse epidemic that's taking too many lives and too much joy from America's teens and college students. There are bigger institutes in the country, but ours is one of a kind. Yes, I'm partial because I helped create it and work there, but trust me, its work and unique approach are desperately needed, since what we have now isn't working.

From anxiety and depression to addiction, eating disorders, and loneliness, American students and families face a mental health and substance misuse epidemic. The William Magee Institute is answering the call by delivering education that spotlights issues individuals, families, and communities confront, while revealing research and solutions. Built upon a culture of compelling storytelling, the Magee Institute uses peer-to-peer student engagement and premium, widely distributed contemporary media. Aimed at deeply connecting and engaging with students and members of their ecosystems, the institute's messaging involves students, parents, educators, and research innovators—all playing a vital role in changing, and even saving, lives and helping students find lasting wellbeing. Our *The Mayo Lab Podcast with David Magee* is a production of the William Magee Institute and its Thomas Hayes Mayo Lab, and it brings together information and education for parents and educators.

We have so many experts and individuals in this country with incredible insight and research into the crisis faced, but this information often lives in silos. Through the Magee Institute, we're bringing this information into entertaining, accessible formats like the podcast. It's named after Thomas Mayo, a college student who died of an accidental drug overdose due to fentanyl poisoning. The podcast's aim: help stop senseless deaths, and stop more from joining the walking dead. Show guests include students, parents, educators, and research innovators, resulting in a program aimed at helping students and families find lasting joy and wellbeing. You can find it on Apple Podcasts, Spotify, Google Podcasts, Audible, Stitcher, and almost everywhere podcasts air. I hope you'll listen and follow us on social media.

Finally, it's worth noting that this book, while written on my time out of the office, is made possible through the enlightenment and support I receive from the William Magee Institute team. They, along with the University of Mississippi leadership, have encouraged me to speak and deliver information to students and parents across the country so that we can help end this epidemic. And you can help us help others. If you'd like to make a donation to the William Magee Institute for Student Wellbeing to support this vital work, including research that paves the way to better outcomes, you can find details on where and how to give at magee.olemiss.edu.

Acknowledgments

I've been fortunate in a book-writing career now spanning two decades to have worked with the top publishing companies in the country, including HarperCollins, Penguin Random House, Wiley, and McGraw Hill. But I must say that the publishing experience on this book, and my previous one, *Dear William: A Father's Memoir of Addiction, Recovery, Love, and Loss*, is my favorite yet. That's because BenBella, which includes the Matt Holt imprint publishing this book, is what I'd call an author's publisher—boutique and approachable while big enough (distributed by Penguin Random House) and successful (multiple bestsellers across several categories).

I'd worked on two books with Matt Holt when he headed the trade division at Wiley, and when he landed his own imprint at BenBella it seemed a natural fit. The experience has been better than I'd hoped, and I've since also sent other authors his way, including my friend John Talty, for his book *The Leadership Secrets of Nick Saban*, which also found wonderful critical and commercial success.

Not long after I submitted *Dear William*, Matt suggested a book for parents on everything they needed to know about substance misuse. I'd written a successful self-help book previously—*How Toyota Became #1*, published by Penguin in 2007, was an English-language business/self-help bestseller in India and still delivers small royalty checks more than fifteen years after publication. So I wasn't intimidated by this writing format, but after *Dear William* received literary acclaim, I wondered if I should back it up with another more literary work. From a writer's perspective, perhaps so. But as someone called to help students and families navigate the mental health and substance misuse crisis, I ultimately decided that this message mattered more than my ego. Sure, every writer wants another crack at delivering a literary work. The truth is, though, that what every writer wants most of all is to have a positive impact on lives.

That's why I'm thankful for Matt Holt and the team at BenBella I work with, including senior editor Katie Dickman, who played a vital role in this book; and senior marketing manager Mallory Hyde.

Beyond BenBella, I'm thankful for my agent, Esmond Harmsworth, president of Aevitas Creative Management, and the talented and supportive team that manages my speaking engagements at APB Speakers.

At the University of Mississippi, I'm appreciative of the steadfast support from many, including Charlotte Parks, Natasha Jeter, Meagen Rosenthal, Brett Barefoot, Shirley Gray, and Alexis Lee.

I'd also never get this or any work done without my family. My wife, Kent, provides a foundation of encouragement and feedback to craft and deliver the message. There are also my two adult children, Hudson and Mary Halley. Each is now married with a family of their own, and they play such valuable supportive roles in my storytelling journey. I'm sure you'll recall anecdotal mentions of them throughout this book, and if you happened to read *Dear William*, my memoir, you got a lot more than tidbits about their lives and recovery. They allow me to tell their stories because they understand how vital that is to helping other students and families.

We do this together as a family because it broke us as a family, and while we healed individually, we also healed collectively. I love them, each and every one, and am thankful they support me in bringing this and other important storytelling to you.

My hope is that you and every member of your family find the same joy and love that sustain us.

A Resource Guide for Parents and Families

Most communities throughout the country have resources available for helping students, parents, and families cope with and better manage mental-health and substance-misuse issues. I'd encourage you to ask professionals, including school counselors, physicians, and therapists, about those that might meet your needs. But I'll also point out some valuable resources for parents and families, which are easily accessible digitally, and some support groups that are national but available through local networks and meetings. It's not a comprehensive list; instead, it's a foundational starting point. You'll find directions to even more helpful resources as you explore each one. And finally, the best help is reaching out to a friend or family member who has experienced addiction, treatment, and recovery of a teen or adult. Most are willing to share resources they know about to help you and your loved one find joy.

PODCASTS

The Mayo Lab Podcast with David Magee (www.themayolab podcast.com) is available on all the major podcast-distribution sites, including Apple Podcasts, Google Podcasts, Audible, and Spotify. This is a new weekly and biweekly podcast I host and launched in early 2023 that focuses solely on everything parents and educators need to know about the student mental-health and wellbeing crisis, including insight from leading researchers and educators who bring forth solutions. It is produced by the William Magee Institute for Student Wellbeing at the University of Mississippi. The Thomas Hayes Mayo Lab is named after a college student I knew who died of an accidental drug overdose from fentanyl.

The *Heart of the Matter* podcast with Elizabeth Vargas (https://drugfree.org/elizabeth-vargas-podcast/) focuses on addiction broadly rather than with teens or students like the *Mayo Lab* podcast does, but it's one of the best resources available to learn from others about the challenges faced and solutions found. Produced by the Partnership to End Addiction, the weekly podcast features guests who have found success in recovery or helped others get there. Elizabeth Vargas is in recovery as well, making her an excellent and insightful host. *Heart of the Matter* is available on all major podcast-distribution sites.

The *My Child & ADDICTION* podcast is a parent-to-parent discussion developed by three fathers whose children struggle with substance use disorder. The fathers are joined by other parents, and they expose support group–type conversations to listeners, revealing stories that parents and families can relate to about challenges faced and what works in supporting recovery and the recovery of those impacted. *My Child & ADDICTION* is available on all major podcast-distribution sites.

CONTENT SITES

The Child Mind Institute (www.childmind.org) is a nonprofit that advances "children's mental health through compassionate and uncompromising clinical care, a revolutionary approach to the science of the developing brain, and wide-reaching public education and community programs," and its website also provides insightful and up-to-date information regarding care, education, and science in the youth mental-health field. It's one of the more useful information sites for parents with questions in the early stages of seeking help.

The Partnership to End Addiction's website (www.drugfree .org) is an excellent site for those looking for answers around prevention, early action, treatment, and recovery. Like its podcast, its content is focused on all ages, but parents and educators will find trustworthy, up-to-date insight and guiding information.

Alcoholics Anonymous (www.aa.org) provides excellent information on its website, including videos for young adults who struggle with substance misuse. AA provides a wide range of videos and information useful throughout the recovery process as well, applicable to all ages, and the site includes assessment surveys for those who think they may have a problem.

The National Institute on Alcohol Abuse and Alcoholism (www.niaaa.nih.gov) is useful with fact-based information that covers basics of how alcohol impacts health and the definition and risks of binge drinking, hangovers, and more. The website delivers information in the manner one might expect from a government entity—parents will find it more useful and interesting than teens will, likely—but its baseline facts are helpful.

Parents and educators who want to find treatment resources to consider or recommend can also use the website's searchable database, revealing programs, doctors, and therapists state by state and community by community throughout the country.

The National Institute on Drug Abuse (www.nida.nih.gov/) has a wealth of science-based information for parents regarding drug use, health impacts, and the developing brain. It's a government website, so users can expect how information is explained, but it's up to date and technically correct in every way, serving as a valuable resource for foundational information.

SUPPORT GROUPS

Alcoholics Anonymous is the community leader in helping individuals find and maintain sobriety from alcohol, and its twelve-step programs exist throughout the world in support. It's a "fellowship of people who come together to solve their drinking problem." Visit www.aa.org and search the site by location to find AA support near you.

Narcotics Anonymous is another support group for those suffering from addiction and seeking recovery, and its community meetings, held throughout the world, are typically found in the same churches and community centers where AA meetings are held. You can find an NA meeting in your community and also participate in virtual NA meetings on the website at www.na.org/.

Since addiction impacts everyone in the family, support groups for loved ones are quite helpful and available in almost every community in the country and many throughout the world. Support groups for adults, including parents and spouses of those suffering from addiction, are available through Al-Anon meetings, while teenagers impacted can engage in support through Alateen groups. According to the Al-Anon Family Groups site, Al-Anon is "a mutual support program for people whose lives have been affected by someone else's drinking. By sharing common experiences and applying the Al-Anon principles, families and friends of alcoholics can bring positive changes to their individual situations, whether or not the alcoholic admits the existence of a drinking problem or seeks help," while Alateen is "a fellowship of young people (mostly teenagers) whose lives have been affected by someone else's drinking whether they are in your life drinking or not. By attending Alateen, teenagers meet other teenagers with similar situations." For more information and a searchable database of meetings in your area, visit www.al-anon.org/.

Notes

INTRODUCTION

1 *"felt sad or hopeless during the past year"*: "New CDC Data Illuminate Youth Mental Health Threats During the COVID-19 Pandemic," Centers for Disease Control and Prevention, March 31, 2002, https://www.cdc.gov /media/releases/2022/p0331-youth-mental-health-covid-19.html

1 *"future wellbeing of our country depends on how"*: "U.S. Surgeon General Issues Advisory on Youth Mental Health Crisis Further Exposed by COVID-19 Pandemic," U.S. Department of Health and Human Services, December 7, 2021, https://www.hhs.gov/about/news/2021/12/07/us-surgeon-general -issues-advisory-on-youth-mental-health-crisis-further-exposed-by-covid -19-pandemic.html

CHAPTER TWO

27 *"I can't sleep."*: Tammy Chang, "It's Not Just You—Politics Is Stressing Out America's Youth," Institute for Healthcare Policy and Innovation, University of Michigan, February 13, 2018, https://ihpi.umich.edu/news /its-not-just-you-politics-stressing-out-americas-youth

27 *"I'm scared for my safety."* Chang, "It's Not Just You."

30 *most teens still identify as religious:* Jeff Diamant and Elizabeth Podrebarac Sciupac, "10 Key Findings About the Religious Lives of U.S. Teens and Their Parents," Pew Research Center, September 10, 2020, https://www.pewresearch .org/fact-tank/2020/09/10/10-key-findings-about-the-religious-lives-of-u-s -teens-and-their-parents/

31 *Never mind that research has shown:* S. Luthar, P. Small, and L. Ciciolla,

"Adolescents from upper middle class communities: Substance misuse and addiction across early adulthood," *Development and Psychopathology* 30, no. 1 (2018): 315-335. doi:10.1017/S0954579417000645

CHAPTER THREE

37 *"Mr. Webb, a laid-back snowboarder and skateboarder"*: Noah Weiland and Margot Sanger-Katz, "Overdose Deaths Continue Rising, with Fentanyl and Meth Key Culprits, *New York Times*, May 11, 2022, https://www.nytimes .com/2022/05/11/us/politics/overdose-deaths-fentanyl-meth.html

37 *Such overdose deaths of young Americans:* "Morbidity and Mortality Weekly Report," Centers for Disease Control and Prevention, December 16, 2022, https://www.cdc.gov/mmwr/volumes/71/wr/mm7150a2.htm

39 *"Consider that in 2015, 32 percent of American eleven-year-olds owned a smartphone"*: "The Common Sense Census: Media Use by Tweens and Teens: New Research Finds YouTube Videos Beat Out TV and Video Games as Entertainment of Choice for Teens and Tweens," Common Sense, October 29, 2019, https://www .commonsensemedia.org/press-releases/the-common-sense-census-media-use -by-tweens-and-teens-new-research-finds-youtube-videos-beat-out-tv-and

40 *"Why else might American kids be anxious other than telephones?"*: Nathaniel Popper, "Panicking About Your Kids' Phones? New Research Says Don't," *New York Times*, January 17, 2020, https://www.nytimes.com/2020/01/17 /technology/kids-smartphones-depression.html

40 *"less than 20 percent of U.S. teens report reading a book"*: "Teens Today Spend More Time on Digital Media, Less Time Reading," American Psychological Association, August 20, 2018, https://www.apa.org/news/press /releases/2018/08/teenagers-read-book

42 *"There is no single cause of body dissatisfaction or disordered eating."*: "Media & Eating Disorders," National Eating Disorders Association, accessed December 5, 2022, https://www.nationaleatingdisorders.org/ media-eating-disorders

43 *"reverse anorexia" or "bigorexia"*: Christina Frank, "Boys and Eating Disorders: They Don't Fit the Stereotype and Are Often Overlooked," Child Mind Institute, September 27, 2021, https://childmind.org/article/boys-and -eating-disorders/

43 *"These boys have all the psychological features of anorexia"*: Frank, "Boys and Eating Disorders."

43 *Signs of male eating disorders:* Frank, "Boys and Eating Disorders."

49 *A study by Common Sense Media revealed:* "New Report Finds Teens Feel Addicted to Their Phones, Causing Tension at Home," Common Sense Media, May 3, 2016, https://www.commonsensemedia.org/press-releases/new-report-finds-teens-feel-addicted-to-their-phones-causing-tension-at-home

51 *Chavarria told the* New York Times: Nellie Bowles, "A Dark Consensus About Screens and Kids Begins to Emerge in Silicon Valley," *New York Times,* October 26, 2018, https://www.nytimes.com/2018/10/26/style/phones-children-silicon-valley.html

50 *the late Apple founder and CEO Steve Jobs, who told* the New York Times *before his death:* Nick Bilton, "Steve Jobs Was a Low-Tech Parent," *New York Times,* September 10, 2014, https://www.nytimes.com/2014/09/11/fashion/steve-jobs-apple-was-a-low-tech-parent.html?_r=0

51 *The nonprofit organization Wait Until 8th operates under the premise:* "Why Wait?," Wait Until 8th, accessed December 5, 2022, https://www.waituntil8th.org/why-wait

51 *High school teacher Tyler Rablin of Sunnyside, Washington, has seen enough:* Tyler Rablin, Twitter post, May 12, 2022, 1:23 PM, https://twitter.com/mr_rablin/status/1524817664513699847

52 *There's also a clear association between alcohol:* Charles Anzalone, "Study: Substance Use in High Schoolers Linked to Insufficient Sleep," University at Buffalo, March 25, 2020, https://www.buffalo.edu/news/releases/2020/03/022.html

52 *Stanford University poll, which indicated that 87 percent:* Ruthann Richter, "Among Teens, Sleep Deprivation an Epidemic," Stanford Medicine, October 8, 2015, https://med.stanford.edu/news/all-news/2015/10/among-teens-sleep-deprivation-an-epidemic.html.

53 *"since the early 1990s, it's been established":* Richter, "Among Teens, Sleep Deprivation an Epidemic."

53 *More than one-third of all teens get only five to six hours of sleep:* Juliann Garey, "Why Are Teenagers So Sleep-Deprived?," Child Mind Institute, accessed December 5, 2022, https://childmind.org/article/teenagers-sleep-deprived/

54 *"It's not just that Facebook, Twitter, Instagram, Tumblr and YouTube are distractions":* Garey, "Why Are Teenagers So Sleep-Deprived?"

CHAPTER FOUR

60 *In 1995, for example:* National Center for Natural Products Research at the University of Mississippi; updated from ElSohly et al., *Biological Psychiatry* 79, no. 7 (April 1, 2016): 613–619.

61   *Oils used in vape pens, for instance, often contain 70 to 90 percent THC:*
     "Vaping Cannabis Produces Stronger Effects than Smoking Cannabis for
     Infrequent Users," Johns Hopkins Medicine, December 4, 2018, https://
     www.hopkinsmedicine.org/news/newsroom/news-releases/vaping-cannabis
     -produces-stronger-effects-than-smoking-cannabis-for-infrequent-users

61   *It's no coincidence that a 2022 study published in the Lancet:* "Vaping Can-
     nabis Produces Stronger Effects."

62   *Marijuana refers to the dried leaves, flowers, stems, and seeds from the* Canna-
     bis sativa: "Talking with Your Teen About Marijuana: Keeping Your Kids Safe,"
     Substance Abuse and Mental Health Services Administration, accessed Decem-
     ber 5, 2022, https://www.samhsa.gov/sites/default/files/TTHY-Marijuana
     -Broch-2020.pdf

67   *"As with tobacco smoke, marijuana":* "Marijuana Facts for Teens," National
     Institute on Drug Abuse, July 2013, https://nida.nih.gov/sites/default/files
     /teens_brochure_2013.pdf?msclkid=72d3abadac6411ec8d761ff7abf8f7c2

73   *But marijuana use and the vaping of marijuana are on the rise:* "Canna-
     bis Use Highest in Legalized States, More So Among Cigarette Smokers,"
     Columbia, Mailman School of Public Health, July 19, 2022, https://www
     .publichealth.columbia.edu/public-health-now/news/cannabis-use-highest
     -legalized-states-more-so-among-cigarette-smokers

75   *The National Institute on Drug Abuse (NIDA) says that marijuana is addic-*
     tive: "Marijuana Facts for Teens."

75   *"Marijuana is linked to school failure":* "Marijuana Facts for Teens."

80   *What, then, are parents to do:* "Study: Surge of Teen Vaping Levels Off, but
     Remains High as of Early 2020," National Institute on Drug Abuse, De-
     cember 15, 2020, https://nida.nih.gov/news-events/news-releases/2020/12
     /study-surge-of-teen-vaping-levels-off-but-remains-high-as-of-early-2020

CHAPTER FIVE

89   *more than 72 percent of college graduates in this country drink alcohol:*
     Megan Brenan, "U.S. Alcohol Consumption on Low End of Recent Read-
     ings," Gallup, August 19, 2021, https://news.gallup.com/poll/353858/alcohol
     -consumption-low-end-recent-readings.aspx

89   *It's no surprise, then, that children today have their first drink on average:* "11
     Facts About Teens and Alcohol," DoSomething.org, accessed December 5, 2022,
     https://www.dosomething.org/us/facts/11-facts-about-teens-and-alcohol

89   *More than 90 percent of all alcohol consumed by young people:* "National

Survey on Drug Use and Health (NSDUH)," Substance Abuse and Mental Health Data Archive, accessed December 5, 2022, https://www.datafiles.samhsa.gov/dataset/national-survey-drug-use-and-health-2018-nsduh-2018-ds0001

90 *The CDC says binge drinking:* "Binge Drinking," Centers for Disease Control and Prevention, November 14, 2022, https://www.cdc.gov/alcohol/fact-sheets/binge-drinking.htm

92 *more than one hundred college and university presidents in this country created the Amethyst Initiative:* "Welcome to the Amethyst Initiative," Amethyst Initiative, accessed December 5, 2022, https://www.theamethyst initiative.org

94 *data from the World Health Organization:* German Lopez, "Europe Has Lower Drinking Ages than the US—and Worse Teen Drinking Problems," *Vox*, January 26, 2016, https://www.vox.com/2016/1/26/10833208/europe-lower-drinking-age

96 *the following factors contribute to teen alcohol use:* "Underage Drinking," National Institute on Alcohol Abuse and Alcoholism, accessed December 5, 2022, https://www.niaaa.nih.gov/publications/brochures-and-fact-sheets/underage-drinking

97 *"A surprising proportion of parents in our study":* "Parents More Lenient About Alcohol with Teens Who Experienced Puberty Early," Penn State, Social Science Research Institute, April 29, 2021, https://ssri.psu.edu/news/parents-more-lenient-about-alcohol-teens-who-experience-puberty-early

98 *"Research shows that people who start drinking before the age of 15":* "Underage Drinking."

100 *"All addictive drugs affect brain pathways involving reward":* "Drug Use Changes the Brain over Time," Learn.Genetics, Genetic Science Learning Center, August 30, 2013, https://learn.genetics.utah.edu/content/addiction/brainchange

CHAPTER SIX

109 *The CDC says that one in five children:* "Data and Statistics on Children's Mental Health," Centers for Disease Control and Prevention, June 3, 2022, https://www.cdc.gov/childrensmentalhealth/data.html

113 *A 2017 study by the American College Health Association found:* "American College Health Association–National College Health Assessment II: Reference Group Executive Summary, Fall 2018," American College Health Association," 2018, https://www.acha.org/documents/ncha/NCHA-II_Fall_2018_Reference_Group_Executive_Summary.pdf

116 *"Holistic, personalized learning is best mediated"*: Jonathan Eckert, *Just Teaching: Feedback, Engagement, and Well-Being for Each Student* (Thousand Oaks, CA: Corwin, 2023).

116 *A report on the 2016 Gallup Student Poll:* "2016 Gallup Student Poll: A Snapshot of Results and Findings," Gallup, 2017, https://www.sac.edu /research/PublishingImages/Pages/research-studies/2016%20Gallup%20 Student%20Poll%20Snapshot%20Report%20Final.pdf

CHAPTER SEVEN

124 *Adderall . . . has a "high potential for abuse . . .":* "Drug Scheduling," United States Drug Enforcement Administration, accessed December 5, 2022, https://www.dea.gov/drug-information/drug-scheduling

124 *40 percent of teens view prescription drugs as safer:* "National Survey on Drug Use and Health," Substance Abuse and Mental Health Services Administration, accessed December 5, 2022, https://www.samhsa.gov/data/data -we-collect/nsduh-national-survey-drug-use-and-health

126 *The DEA revealed in 2021:* "DEA Highlights 2021," United States Drug Enforcement Administration, 2021, https://www.dea.gov/dea-highlights-2021

130 *Consider that in 2021 the DEA alone confiscated:* "Counterfeit Pills Fact Sheet," Drug Enforcement Administration, accessed January 9, 2023, https:// www.dea.gov/sites/default/files/2021-12/DEA-OPCK_FactSheet_December %202021.pdf

131 *Popular Counterfeit Drugs Internet Search Questions:* "Most Searched Questions: Counterfeit Pills," Just Think Twice, accessed January 9, 2023, https:// www.justthinktwice.gov/facts/most-searched-questions-counterfeit-pills

133 *The flow of fentanyl into the U.S.:* "Fentanyl Flow to the United States," DEA Intelligence Report, January 2020, https://www.dea.gov/sites/default /files/2020-03/DEA_GOV_DIR-008-20%20Fentanyl%20Flow%20in%20 the%20United%20States_0.pdf

134 *"There was a change in consumption, there was a change":* Associated Press, "Mexican Cartels Are Turning to Meth and Fentanyl Production," NPR, December 21, 2021, https://www.npr.org/2021/12/21/1066163872 /mexican-cartels-turning-to-meth-and-fentanyl-production

134 *"China-Mexico law enforcement cooperation against":* Vanda Felbab-Brown, "China and Synthetic Drugs Control: Fentanyl, Methamphetamines, and Precursors," Brookings, March 2022, https://www.brookings.edu/research /china-and-synthetic-drugs-control-fentanyl-methamphetamines-and-precursors/

CHAPTER EIGHT

143 *Defining Substance Use Disorder and Addiction:* "How to Identify Substance Use Disorder & Addiction," Partnership to End Addiction, October 2022, https://drugfree.org/article/how-to-identify-substance-use-disorder-addiction/

156 *Consider that the CDC says that almost 17 percent:* "Binge Drinking," Centers for Disease Control and Prevention, accessed January 9, 2023, https://www.cdc.gov/alcohol/fact-sheets/binge-drinking.htm

CHAPTER NINE

162 *"Children rely on parents to provide them with":* "Parenting Matters," Centers for Disease Control and Prevention, February 22, 2021, https://www.cdc.gov/ncbddd/childdevelopment/features/parenting-matters.html.

162 *In a 2022 study, Columbia University's Mailman School of Public Health:* "Major Uptick Reported in Cannabis Vaping for All Adolescents," Columbia, Mailman School of Public Health, May 19, 2022, https://www.publichealth.columbia.edu/public-health-now/news/major-uptick-reported-cannabis-vaping-all-adolescents

167 *"A parent with a SUD [substance use disorder], who is mood altered":* Laura Lander, Janie Howsare, and Marilyn Byrne, "The Impact of Substance Use Disorders on Families and Children: From Theory to Practice," *Social Work in Public Health* 28, nos. 3–4 (2013): 194–205, https://www.ncbi.nlm.nih.gov/pmc/articles/PMC3725219/#:~:text=A%20parent%20with%20a%20SUD,opportunities%20to%20foster%20healthy%20attachment

CHAPTER TEN

178 *A 2016–2017 University of Michigan survey revealed:* "Fact Sheet: Loneliness on Campus," Project UnLonely, accessed December 5, 2022, https://www.artandhealing.org/campus-loneliness-fact-sheet/

About the Author

David Magee is the award-winning author of *Dear William: A Father's Memoir of Addiction, Recovery, Love, and Loss*—which became a *Publishers Weekly* bestseller, was named a Best Book of the South, and was featured on *CBS Mornings*—and other nonfiction books. A change maker in student and family mental health and substance misuse who speaks in schools throughout the country to students, educators, and parents, he is creator and director of operations of the William Magee Institute for Student Wellbeing at the University of Mississippi and a frequent K–12 and university educational and motivational speaker, helping students and parents find and keep their joy. He is also a national recovery adviser for the Integrative Life Network. Learn more at www.daviddmagee.com.